Harold Horton

The Gifts Of The Spirit

Radiant BOOKS

Gospel Publishing House/Springfield, Mo. 65802

02-0504

Introduction

TODAY there are several books on the Gifts of the Spirit written by Pentecostal brethren. Years ago, when the notes which form the basis of these studies were complete, there was no such book in existence. Over a period of several years in the Women's Bible School of which Howard Carter was the overseer, these studies were taken by me before the students in substance as they stand.

I hope I have provided a book to read, rather than a somewhat savourless text book. Since the book, however, remains a group of serious studies on a much neglected though most important and thoroughly delightful subject, the rudiments of a framework will be found throughout the pages, in some leading thoughts numbered and lettered to facilitate reference.

The studies have really arisen out of the most happy acquaintance I made many years ago with Mr. Howard Carter, of the Bible School and Missionary Association, Hampstead London.

Years of Bible study and meditation and prayer and preaching on the subject have crystallized the studies into their present form.

Incidentally the book contains, so far as I know, the first complete commentary for Pentecostal people on the critical chapters Twelve, Thirteen and Fourteen of First Corinthians.

Perhaps this book may be used of God to lead some thirsty seeker such as I was into the blessedness of the supernatural Canaan that I entered by the Baptism in the Holy Spirit years ago, That to me would be the greatest joy of all. For that joy I would ever bless the Name of the Lord Jesus, and of the Father, and of the Holy Ghost, the Triune Author of the precious Gifts of the Spirit.

H. H., *May* 1934.

These signs shall follow them that believe; in my name they shall cast out devils; they shall speak with new tongues; they shall take up serpents; and if they drink any deadly thing, it shall not hurt them; they shall lay hands on the sick, and they shall recover. Mark xvi, 17, 18.

He that believeth on me, the works that I do shall he do also; and greater works than these shall he do . . . John xiv, 12.

Behold, I send the promise of my Father upon you; but tarry ye in the city of Jerusalem, until ye be endured with power from on high. Luke xxiv, 49.

Ye shall receive power after that the Holy Ghost is come upon you. Acts I, 8.

And they were all filled with the Holy Ghost, and began to speak with other tongues, as the Spirit gave them utterance. Acts ii, 4. *act 2 : 4*

The Lord working with them, and confirming the word with signs following. Mark xvi, 20.

And Stephen, full of faith and power did great wonders and miracles among the people. Acts vi, 8.

And the people with one accord gave heed unto those things which Philip spake, hearing and seeing the miracles which he did, Acts viii, 6.

Grant unto thy servants, that with all boldness they may speak thy word, by stretching forth thine hand to heal; and that signs and wonders may be done by the name of thy holy child Jesus . . . and they spake the word with boldness . . . And by the hands of the apostles were many signs and wonders wrought among the people. Acts iv, 29-31; v, 12.

God also bearing them witness, both with signs and wonders, and with divers miracles, and *Gifts of the Holy Ghost* . . . Heb. ii, 4.

Concerning *Spiritual Gifts*, brethren I would not have you ignorant . . . There are diversities of Gifts, but the same Spirit. . . . Covet earnestly the best Gifts . . . Desire Spiritual Gifts. . . . Covet to prophesy and forbid not to speak with tongues. 1 Cor. xii, 1, 4, 31; xiv, 39.

Contents

1 Signs and Wonders 7

2 Signs and Wonders in Both Testaments 10

3 One Corinthians Twelve 19

4 The Word of Knowledge 39

5 The Word of Wisdom 54

6 Discerning of Spirits 69

7 One Corinthians Thirteen 79

8 The Gifts of Healing 94

9 The Working of Miracles 107

10 The Gift of Faith 119

11 Speaking With Tongues 131

12 Interpretation of Tongues 147

13 Prophecy 158

14 One Corinthians Fourteen 177

15 Signs and Wonders and Reactions 193

16 The Need Today 202

CHAPTER ONE

Signs and Wonders

The redeemed of the Lord are not only saved unto everlasting life; they are the children of God. When we say we are the children of God and that God is our Father we are not merely employing terms of inspiration or endearment, we are not making sentimental nor even devout reference to One who has in marvellous condescension taken up towards us an attitude of benevolence and loving-kindness. When we say that God is our Father and that we are His children, we are using terms of absolute relationship. We are not merely accepted of God: we are begotten of God, Our relationship to God is not one of divine courtesy but of divine life. We are born of God. Our divine Parentage is as real as, but infinitely more enduring than, our human parentage. As children of God we are partakers—now—of His mighty, miraculous super-nature. Beloved, now are we the sons of God, partakers of His divine nature. (2 Peter i, 4; 1 John iii, 2.)

The message of the whole of Scripture is that this miraculous super-nature of God should be manifest in His children. Like Father like son. And God has made full provision for the manifestation of that super-nature in His Children in the Gifts of the Holy Spirit.

Again, we are not only co-heirs with the Lord Jesus, by virtue of which relationship He is not ashamed to call us brethren (Heb, ii,11): we are said to be the children of the Lord (Heb. ii, 13), born of Him, the incorruptible Seed, the eternal, Living Word. As children of the Lord we are possessors of His very nature and ought as such to display evidence in our measure not only of His perfect character but of His mighty divine faculties. We are the sons and daughters of

7

THE GIFTS OF THE SPIRIT

Omnipotence and Omniscience, as well as of Infinite Holiness
and Endless Life. The off-spring of a bird displays every
bird-like faculty and characteristic. The moment they are born
they are miniature copies of their parents. They eat, breathe,
move, think, like a bird. There comes a time when, like a bird,
they spread tentative wings and take to the air. The son of a
bird can fly! It can also sing. The offspring of an earth-born
creature cannot fly: nor sing. It has the wrong nature. The
heaven-born sons of God should evince heavenly, that is
super-natural, beyond-natural, characteristics. God has
provided in the baptism of the Holy Spirit and the resultant
Gifts of the Spirit, means for the reproduction of His divine
faculties in His children.

Now the heavenly super-nature of the Lord Jesus was
manifested not in the carpenter's shop at Nazareth, for there,
during the whole of His young manhood, in common with all
the carpenter-fellows of His day, He wrought the objects of
His trade by human skill and by the use of ordinary material
tools. The marvellous fabric of His spotless daily life He also
wrought through the faith and the Word that were available to
the men and women round about Him. His divine super-nature
was manifested in His miraculous works wrought by those
heaven-given tools, the Gifts of the Holy Spirit, with which He
was endowed immediately on His receiving the baptism of the
Holy Spirit on that memorable day in Jordan (Matt, iii, 16).
The Scripture is scarcely more insistent on any subject than on
this—that the children of God should express at least in some
fragmentary measure this divine miraculous super-nature. For
this reason both the Lord Jesus and His children are said in the
Prophets to be "for signs and for wonders" (Isaiah viii, 18).
This supernatural divine power and wisdom was seen in
unmistakable manifestation in His simple children immediately
after their baptism in the Holy Ghost on the day of Pentecost.
It was not a theological claim that arrested the devout Jews on
that memorable day, but a manifestation of divine wisdom and
power in the speaking of miraculous tongues by unlearned
followers of the Lord Jesus. It was not a masterly unfolding of

8

the Word that set the envious priests by the ears some time later, but a mighty and immediate operation of the Gifts of the Spirit in a lame-born man by two of the simple children of God. It was not a phenomenal display of evangelical fervour that swept Samaria some time later still, but a repeated demonstration of the Gifts of the Spirit in supernatural healings, through the Spirit-filled hands of one who was not considered capable of ministering the Word of God, (Acts viii, 6; vi, 2-4.) Neither was it alone the sweet savour of fragrant holiness in Paul that caused the astounded Lycaonians and the gentle-hearted Maltese barbarians to ascribe to him divine origin and rank, but an unanswerable display of divine power through the Gifts of the Spirit in miracle after miracle of human deliverance (Acts xiv, 3, 11; xxviii, 6).

In regeneration the Lord Jesus has stamped upon His begotten ones the impress of His life and loveliness. In the baptism of the Spirit He has designed to charge them with His heavenly dynamic. In the Gifts of the Spirit He has provided for the visible, audible and tangible expression of that dynamic, in the utterance of things that transcend profoundest human thought, and in the doing of things that surpass the utmost human skill, "Behold, I and the children whom the Lord hath given me, are for signs and for wonders."

CHAPTER TWO

Signs and Wonders in Both Testaments

It will be admitted by all that God's faculties are constant, that His attributes are eternal, His abilities immutable. God has not evolved nor is He evolving. God always IS. God is not growing in grace or wisdom or power, as His children are encouraged to do. His power and wisdom are this day what they were before the morning stars sang together. The fires that forged the strong bands of Orion are the same as smote Abihu, licked Elijah's trenches, floodlit Horeb's mercy seat, rose in amber gusts before the rapt Ezekiel, sat in tongues upon Peter and Mary, blinded the eyes of Saul of Tarsus, flamed in the Judaean dungeon—the same that shall clothe Emmanuel from the appearance of His loins upward and from the appearance of His loins downward a thousand millenniums to be.

God will never be what He is not, and what He ever was He is. He has not developed in Himself. His power, wisdom, presence are ever the same. The Bible does not give us a revelation of God's growing power or knowledge. God's energies do not grow—they change not. It is not God's power that has changed from dispensation to dispensation, but the incidence of that power and the manner of its communication. The New Testament Lord is the same as the Old Testament Lord. But the revelation of God's contacts and dealings with men is more glorious since His Son came to blazon Him forth, and the mode of communication of His glory is different since His Holy Spirit came with us to dwell.

Now the Gifts of the Spirit are a new thing since the commencement of the Holy Ghost dispensation on the Day of Pentecost, but the power behind them is older than the conquests of Gideon or the plagues of Egypt. Right away,

10

therefore, it may be said with the concurrence of the reader that all God's works of wisdom or power in any age are operations either of the Gifts of the Spirit or of the Spirit behind the Gifts in one or other of His temporary supernatural manifestations. Or, passing the contradiction in terms, may it not be said that the miracles of the Old Testament were wrought through the loan of one or more of the Gifts of the Spirit, while the miracles in the New Testament, and the thousands that are bing witnessed today, are wrought through the loan of that same power being now freely distributed as a Gift?

My father had a nice watch that he promised me should be mine at his death. But since "he liked me," to do me some loving service (and impatient to see me enjoying his watch while it was his), during the later years of his life he lent me his watch and bequeathed it to me at his decease. During his life, therefore, he reserved to himself the right of withdrawing the watch either for his own use or that of one of his other sons. At the moment of writing it is in my pocket, my own property, most efficiently serving my needs every day. My father has long ago entered into that timeless realm whose rolling ages are marked in shadowless beams from the lovely irradiant face of his Saviour. But his watch that was once a loan is a gift. In the Old Testament the Lord Jesus in His word often promised His children that He would one day give them the Gifts of His blessed Spirit (Joel ii, 28). That glorious presentation should be made after the death that He must die for them. But since "He liked them" to show them forth already as His children, and was, so to speak, anxious that they should possess ornaments to decorate them and instruments to bless them, even before He should lay down His mighty life for them, He loaned certain of them the Gifts from the days of their bondage in Egypt and bequeathed them as Gifts after His eventual decease. Up to His decease He reserved to Himself the right of withdrawing the loan or transferring it temporarily to some other of His sons. But He has gone up on high, shedding forth glorious things that may be seen and heard, giving gifts

11

unto men, unto all that will receive them, Gifts that are daily operative in enlightenment and deliverances, Gifts that are without repentance.

Or to present the same thought in rather a different way—in the old dispensation revelation and power were imposed by God at His sovereign will upon chosen agents, while today they are exercised, still at His sovereign will, by those in possession of the Gifts of the Spirit.

I remember reading some years ago in the daily paper of some wonderful experiments that were carried out in the Albert Hall in London. An electrical scientist was demonstrating his invention. It was in the form of a miniature dirigible airship not more than a foot in length, to judge by the photographs reproduced in the newspaper. Now, this marvellous little instrument was launched into the air in that huge auditorium before the astonished gaze of the thousands of scientists who had gathered to see it. Steadying itself for a moment it started on its silent, mysterious trip. Round the hall it soared at the level of the first balcony; then, taking an upward turn as if by an act of its own volition, it reversed at the level of the second balcony and circumnavigated the hall in an opposite direction. Up once more it nosed, and reaching the third balcony, steered a straight course from front to back of the hall. Upward once more and back again, traversing its invisible path. Then some startling gyrations and convolutions in mid-air when from some secret chamber of its sensitive frame were launched a series of miniature bombs upon the heads of the astonished beholders! Up and down again, as if impelled by some mystic "brain" secreted somewhere in the midst of its fragile structure. Everywhere in that vast hall it steered in mysterious ascent, dip or glide, round and back again "as the governor listed." And yet there was no govenor on board—no powers of propulsion or direction or manipulation in its complex organism, But in the topmost gallery of the hall the creative scientist with an electrical apparatus emitting invisible rays of galvanic power, which, operating on the "organs" of the dirigible, sent it hither and thither at the

12

will of the maker, wise beyond its wisdom, and able beyond its ability. The "govenor who listed" in a word, was present, not on board, but in the lofty dome of the building, working his pleasure upon the little creation of his mind beneath him.

In the Old Testament days the Governor, the Holy Spirit, was aloft in the heavens, operating as He would from His headquarters in the glory. "And the Spirit of the Lord came upon David from that day forward," urging him through the valley of Elah, guiding him in the selection of those ordinarily futile pebbles, now become divinely drenched fragments of Omnipotence, pressing upon him words to amaze the king and a humble challenge to engage the enraged Philistinian giant; giving force and direction to the stone, laying low the boaster and exalting the humble shepherd. All this by the energy of an illumination and a power from heaven that clothed him expressly for the exploit.

Have you seen the stately airships attached to the British Navy? One summer evening in company with my wife and my brother, I saw a mighty "dirigible" sailing over Hammersmith, steering and soaring high in the blue, whithersoever the governor listed. This time the commander and propelling apparatus were aboard the ship. At the commander's will it rose or descended, turned or straightened out, sped or hovered. At his will went messages of communication between headquarters and the crew. At his will, as occasion might need, aerial torpedoes could descend or smoke-cloud arise; at his behest coded words of counsel or protection might proceed for the benefit of the earth-dwellers beneath. Thus out of the fragile craft proceeded, as it were, magnetic rays of wisdom and galvanic emanations of irresistible power at the will of the hidden director and the need of the people below.

On the Day of Pentecost—to retain the figure—the Governor came down from heaven to earth and entered the "dirigible" bodies and minds of the redeemed (I Cor. vi, 19). Today He operates on board our hearts: thus emanations of supernatural enlightenment and might are manifested "as He will." The instruments and means of distribution of this

13

heavenly wisdom and energy are the Gifts of the Holy Spirit. The Commander is the same as ever. His centre of operations is transferred from heaven to earth; His mode of communication is changed from without to within. In the olden days God's precious things were ministered to men by the Holy Ghost situate in heaven. Since Pentecost's outpouring those same mighty "things" are ministered to us by "the Holy Ghost sent down from heaven" (I Peter 1, 12). In the old dispensation the Holy Ghost came mightily upon men; in the new He dwells mightily within them. That is the exact difference in the signification of the prepositions employed by the Lord in John xiv, 17, "He is *with* you [before Pentecost]: He shall be *in* you [after Pentecost]." In the old dispensation men experienced divine power; in the new they received power. In the old they responded to power; in the new He gives them power (Luke x, 19). The Holy Ghost descended upon men before Pentecost; today, since that heaven-descending cloudburst; He saturates and fills them (Acts ii, 4; i, 8).

This truth is abundantly illustrated in the Scriptures. In the corrupt days of the Judges, when back-slidden Israel cried unto the Lord for deliverance from enemy oppression, "the Spirit of the Lord came upon "Othniel, pressing upon him heaven's revelation for rulership, and heaven's supernatural power for victory over the arrogant Mesopotamian monarch. Years later, during another enemy conquest, "the Spirit of the Lord came upon" a farm hand (Judges vi, 34) who with a helpless handful of three hundred, and with no strategy save that dictated from heavenly headquarters by the Spirit, discomfited a host of trained Midianites like grasshoppers for multitude, and like the sands of the sea innumerable (Judges vii, 12). Still later, under yet another enemy conquest, "the Spirit of the Lord came upon" a despised and proscribed "son of a harlot" (Judges xi, 29). He smote the mighty Ammonites "from Aroer, even until thou come to Minnith, with a very great slaughter, and the Lord delivered them into his hands."

Later still, as the bitter fruit of yet another apostasy, the giant hordes rushed out of the Philistinian cities of Ekron,

Gaza, Ashdod, Gath, over-running and over-powering the children of Israel. "The Spirit of the Lord came upon" an obscure and undistinguished Danite. Unarmed and single-handed he slew thirty ponderous giants out of Ashkelon and stripped them of their garments for his uses (Judges xiv, 19). Again "the Spirit of the Lord came mightily upon him." The tough cords that bound him flew like tindered flax; with a ludicrous weapon he turned Ramath-Lehi into a charnel field, leaving it strewn with the carcases of "heaps upon heaps" of Philistinian monsters (Judges xv, 14). "The Spirit of the Lord came mightily upon him" at Timnath: he laid his anointed hand upon a lion—not as one who with desperate force engages in mortal combat, but as one who with less than normal effort tears limb from limb an unresisting kid. "He had nothing in his hand": the weapon was in the hand of God, wielded by the Spirit.

These instances are limited to one book of the Bible. There are numerous others. These, however, will suffice to show that in the old dispensation God's energies were imposed from heaven upon chosen individuals for specific leadings and deliverances. In the new dispensation those energies are dis-tributed among men—to all who will believe for them, to all that are "afar off," for the manifestation of the Spirit is given to every man to profit withal—distributed in the form of Gifts to be operated generally speaking by the possessor at the will of the Spirit. The Greek word *charism* (gift), employed five times in this twelfth chapter of One Corinthians, leaves no doubt about God's intention. Its import is inescapable when it is used to characterize the life we have in Jesus Christ. "The charism of God is eternal life through Jesus Christ our Lord," says Paul to the Romans.

Observe Peter employing one of these Gifts at the Beautiful Gate of the Temple. "The gifts you crave," he says in effect to the impotent man, "I am as destitute of as you. But I am not destitute. I have something. In my personal possession. I give you that. It is better than the gold you seek. It is power for your instant healing. In the Name of Jesus Christ of Nazareth

15

rise up and walk." He uses his gift as one in conscious possession of it. With humble confidence and fearless authority he imparts what he has. Not "O Lord, if it be Thy will, raise up this man." But, "Man. look on us! We have something for you from Jesus! Rise and walk!" Blessed Gifts of the Spirit for the lifting of the helpless! Who could not be poor in material goods and natural talents if he might thus be rich in heavenly power for the mending of broken humanity! "Heal the sick," says the Lord to His followers. Not "Ask me and I will heal them." "Cast out demons, cleanse the lepers, raise the dead." Yes, even in the solemn chamber of the beloved dead, "turning to the body, Peter said, Tabitha arise" (Acts ix, 40). Not turning to the heavens crying, "Lord raise her!" Turning to the dead, saying, Arise! "I give you power, Raise the dead," said the Lord. Surcharged in his inward parts with the Spirit's conquering vitality, Peter seizes his God-given authority "by force, snatching it" as his Lord instructed him (Matt. xi, 12), and looking at the dead, with no mention of heaven's mightest Name, but in the power of the Mighty One behind the Name, he says, "Rise."

So also Paul at Lystra. Overflowing with a glorious assurance of partnership with his Father and part ownership with His mighty Son in the all-conquering infinities of the Spirit, steadfastly beholding that life-long cripple among the festooned and futile idols of ancient Greece—with no audible invocation of the Name, but in conscious possession of the authority with which that Name had already invested him, "said with a loud voice, Stand upright on thy feet; and he leaped and walked."

Paul longs, furthermore, to see the Romans that he might impart to them some spiritual gift (Romans i, 11). Not that he might encourage them to pray for some gift, nor that he might seek God on their behalf for such impartation. Intensely conscious of those spiritual gifts which are the necessary accompaniment of the Holy Ghost within him, he longs to "impart a share of" what he has. For no man, be he tentmaker or archbishop, can ever impart what he has not, though he pretend it with all the pomp and paraphernalia of authorized sacerdotalism.

It is an incontestable Scripture revelation that God designs that His children shall be, as it were, purveyors of heaven's bright and glorious commodities. His children, to repeat, are for signs and wonders. In the Old Testament days certain individuals; in the New Age since Pentecost, ALL may possess some blessed "administration" of the Holy Ghost for the edification of the Church and the benefit of the suffering world. In the Old Testament *some* are for signs and wonders wrought by the Holy Ghost from heaven. In the New Testament ALL are for signs and wonders wrought by the Holy Ghost from within them. Before Pentecost Elijah in the presence of the dead looked up to God and cried, "O Lord, I pray thee, let this child's soul come into his inward parts again." Elisha in the Shunammite's house, went into the chamber of the dead, and looking up to heaven "prayed unto the Lord." After Pentecost Peter, turning not to heaven, but to the insentient body of the beloved Dorcas, spoke his Spirit-given word of authority, "Rise!" She opened her eyes, moved, spoke, rose, "Ye shall receive power after that the Holy Ghost is come upon you." And as with the Gift of Miracles or Faith, so with the remaining eight. He hath shed forth This resulting in These, that all the redeemed might covet them and receive them and employ them fearlessly, as He did in Capernaum and Cana and Jerusalem and Sidon, that His ministry of complete redemption for spirit, soul and body may be continued with equal and even increased power through the anointed hands of His blood-purchased children (John xiv, 12).

The loving Father was anxious in the old days that all "the world of sinners lost," as well as His own beloved people, should enjoy manifestations of His living presence in their midst. "The Lord said unto Moses, When thou goest into Egypt, see thou do all those wonders before Pharaoh which I have put in thine hand" (Exodus iv, 21). "And the Lord showed signs and wonders great and sore upon Egypt—before our eyes" (Deut. vi, 22; vii, 19). So right through the ages holy men have found themselves, like Micah, "truly full of power by the Spirit of the Lord." So also in the new age, in consonance with His unchanging design, God bears witness both with signs and wonders and with divers gifts of the Holy Ghost, according to HIS own will (Heb. ii, 4). granting signs and wonders to be done by redeemed hands (Acts xiv, 3) in fulfilment of His own most gracious promise (Mark xvi, 20), that the peoples for whom He died might know by incontrovertible demonstration that He is a Saviour, a Deliverer, a loving friend and a sovereign Lord.

CHAPTER THREE

One Corinthians Twelve

When a geologist or an agriculturist is taking specimens of earth for analysis he does well to include in his survey a wide territory of surrounding country. An examination of isolated specimens does not give the true character of the land.

Much confusion has been wrought in Bible exposition and much damage done to Christianity, by the careless habit of concentrating on an isolated verse of Scripture, with no proper reference to its relationships. The context is often a sufficient commentary on a difficult verse. No solitary, minute portion can be expected to yield its meaning without a full consideration of its illuminating surroundings.

The enumeration of Spiritual Gifts is limited to a few verses in One Corinthians Twelve, but to understand them fully a careful survey must be made of a generous portion of this precious epistle.

Reviewing the five chapters, Ten to Fourteen, it will be noticed that some phase or other of Christian conduct is dealt with in all of them, with special emphasis on believers' behaviour in the Christian assembly—what we today call the Believers' Meeting.

Chapter Ten shows that God's people in the olden days had services and ordinances corresponding to our sacraments and disciplines today. They were all baptized in type as they passed through the Red Sea and annointed as they dwelt under the cloud; they partook of the table of the Lord in the manna and the Rock and the altar, and were subjects of innumerable miracles as they passed through the wilderness, Yet God was

19

displeased with them because of their behaviour in respect of these ordinances, so to speak: for they were neither grateful nor orderly in their worship and work, nor were they even believing in the enjoyment of their daily miracles of provision and guidance and victory.

Chapter Eleven comes to closer grips with the subject of worship in Christian assemblies, showing the manner of dress in men and women, and the general deportment that is acceptable to God in our Breaking of Bread meeting.

Chapters Twelve to Fourteen deal more particularly with the believers' supernatural equipment for service and worship, in the various Gifts of the Spirit, and the emphasis is again on the meeting for worship, or the Believers' Meeting, where certain of the Gifts are especially designed to be in evidence. There can be no fully acceptable conformity to God's pattern of divine worship in a church where Spiritual Gifts are despised, or neglected, or abused. Spiritual Gifts are not an option in the Word. They are a positive essential not only to service but also to worship. They are necessary avenues of revelation and necessary vehicles of adoration without which no meeting for divine worship can be complete. They are, in addition, necessary instruments of power in service. With all our claims to godliness and all our loyalty to the ordinances and sacraments, we too, like the Israelites of old, shall fail to please God, not only if the dynamics of our worship are without orderliness, but also if our strict orderliness in worship or service is without power and supernatural accompaniments.

1 Now concerning spiritual gifts, brethren, I would not have you ignorant.

Plainly God's intention is that His people should be enlightened concerning the miraculous Gifts of the Spirit. The ignorance of Christendom concerning these blessed agents of Christly blessing is nothing short of appalling. In more than thirty years' close association with the Methodist Church I do not recall hearing one solitary reference to these chapters twelve and fourteen of First Corinthians. God would not have such ignorance in His people. And notice that the ignorance that Paul by the Spirit is challenging is not ignorance concerning the existence of the Gifts, for these Corinthians knew well about them and were in enjoyment of them; but ignorance concerning their uses, employment and control. If the condition of these Greeks, in a church which was in possession of all the nine Gifts in regular operation, is described as "ignorant," by what word could the Christian Church of today be suitably characterized! It is Scriptural not to hide away these Gifts from the anxious scrutiny of hungry questioners, but to bring them out into the full light and examine them in the Word by the powerful lens of the Spirit, their Author.

2 Ye know that ye were Gentiles, carried away unto these dumb idols, even as ye were led.
3 Wherefore I give you to understand, that no man speaking by the Spirit of God calleth Jesus accursed; and that no man can say that Jesus is the Lord, but by the Holy Ghost.

The Corinthians as citizens of a Gentile city were formerly hopeless idolaters. As such they were familiar, as all idolatrous peoples are today, with supernatural powers and their operations. For not only among the Gentiles in such cities, but even among the Jews, there were exorcists and magicians and wizards and sorcerers, all as spiritists today, soothsaying and exorcising and miracle-working under the influence of supernatural power—satanic supernatural power. Even their idols were deified demons (x, 20), through which, though they were "nothing in the world," Satan worked miracles by hypnotic suggestion, as in Pharaoh's day.

These Gentile converts must not be ignorant of the fundamental difference between such manifestations and the authentic supernatural manifestations of the Spirit of God. If any man "calleth Jesus accursed," let his miracles be ever so numerous or mighty, let his claims to be under the influence of the Holy Spirit be ever so insistent or impressive, he is a wicked impostor: he is an agent of the Devil.

On the other hand, those Christians whose lives and voices proclaim that they acknowledge the lordship of Jesus will be accepted in their supernatural manifestations as under the authentic inspiration of the Spirit of God.

The point to bear in mind here is that Paul is writing to those who without undue astonishment were living in an atmosphere charged with the supernatural, where miracles were a daily occurrence, where such manifestations were expected, and where counterfeits of spiritist origin were—as ever before or since during heaven's blessed outpourings—in strong and insistent evidence. It is sad to contemplate that all Christendom today is familiar with the adversary's counterfeits in spiritism and "christian science," and yet in the main is busy rejecting heaven's beneficent outpourings and even calumniating those who seek to promote them. It is not strange that in these latter days of Holy Ghost revelation the crawling rods of Jannes and Jambres should swallow up the miracle-rod of Aaron? Has Moses bowed the knee to Pharaoh? Has the almighty adversary usurped real ascendancy over the Almighty? To look at the power and prevalence of occultism in the world today, and the naked futility of the Church of God, one would think some new Simon Magus has substantiated his claim to greatness, beggaring Jehovah with his modern issue of sorceries; that evil Barjesus had out-divined Divinity by his devilish subtleties, openly defying the Holy Ghost that once blinded him. Must the prophet of the Lord now cut himself in vain, calling upon an empty heaven, while Baal produces spurious fire for the deception of his worshippers and the beloved people of God? Must a Gideon come once more from the wheat fields into the carpeted aisles of our churches to repeat in the unbelieving ears of the professionals his sorrowful challenge, "If the Lord be with us, why then is all this befallen us? and where be all His miracles?" And has not this same Gideon arisen in the unsophisticated Pentecostal movement, that has thrust its little fleece together, and "wringed" out a bowlful of heavenly dew upon the dust of modern barrenness, and blown its challenging blast in the ears of the boastful foes of the Lord?

4 Now there are diversities of gifts, but the same Spirit.

5 And there are differences of administrations, but the same Lord.

6 And there are diversities of operations, but it is the same God which worketh all in all.

7 But the manifestation of the Spirit is given to every man to profit withal.

The gifts are diverse and the Giver One. The streams are many, the Source is One. Or the River is One and full of water: the streams thereof are nine; they assuredly make glad the city of God!

The variety of the Spirit's operations is the variety not of division but of unity. The diversity is corporate not competitive; the variety, not of stars that are flying asunder from one another, though they appear in the same night sky, but of the multicoloured rays that stream from the noon sun, all centred in One Orb because all emanating from the One Orb: the differences of administration are not for individual exaltation but for corporate power.

And some Gift of the Spirit is bestowed upon "every man." Not every man who is born. Not every man who is born again, for we must twice limit the circle; but every man who is filled with the Spirit as these Corinthians were. How many Christians would even claim that they have a miraculous endowment for service?

Most of them are really alarmed at the very words "miracle, sign, wonder"! The Gifts of the Spirit are the outward evidence of the indwelling Spirit in those who are baptized in the Spirit. In Rome, you remember there was a fine church, long-established and far-famed, yet until Paul arrived among them they were not generally baptized in the Holy Ghost, and therefore not generally endowed with the Gifts of the Spirit. Paul longed to see them that he might impart to them some spiritual gift (Romans i, 8, 11).

8 For to one is given by the Spirit the word of wisdom; to another the word of knowledge by the same Spirit;

9 To another faith by the same Spirit; to another the gifts of healing by the same Spirit;

10 To another the working of miracles; to another prophecy; to another discerning of spirits; to another divers kinds of tongues; to another the interpretation of tongues:

11 But all these worketh that one and the self-same Spirit, dividing to every man severally as he will.

23

In the baptism in the Spirit the Holy Ghost has not only stepped down from heaven to earth: He has also divided His omnipotence and omniscience into nine more or less equal parts for distribution among the children of the Lord. God hath shined upon men with the diverse rays of His multiform power. His ultra-activities and infra-vision, so to speak, like the invisible activities at the extremities of the spectrum, have fallen on the hearts of simple men and women. For Pentecost applied a prism to the Spirit's heavenly energies, casting a glowing spectrum of nine gracious elements upon this sin-darkened earth, making available God's power for its needs and deliverances. Glorious beams of heavenly splendour, radiant, incandescent, mighty; disease-withering beams, demon-destroying beams, sight-giving, tongue-loosening, mind-illuminating, life-infusing, thirst-quenching, heart-gladdening, soul-reviving beams. What shall the people of God put in the place of these salutary galvanic beams while the world is employing its Röntgen rays and violet rays and radio-activities and other artificialities of power? Shall the Church of God be content with the metaphor in place of the might, the coloured windows and altar lamps instead of the omnipotent energies of the Holy Spirit? Shall we not by wondrous grace restore to the suffering world the healing instead of the haloed Christ, the mighty instead of the mitred apostles, the unctionized instead of the canonized messengers of the Gospel of complete redemption? Not by might—of multitude or organization; not by power—of position, or culture, or science; but by my Spirit, saith the Lord of Hosts. The energies of the unchanging Spirit are still available for earth's desperate needs at the desire of the humble.

I have seen heaven's coloured light playing on baby hands, cast from a cluster ornament interposed between the rays of the sun. Heaven's glory in the hands of a babe! Precious ninefold cluster for this dark world's illumining.

The roseate beam fell once on baby lips: the golden slendour alighted on infant eyes. By that prophetic light the unlearned eyes recognized the King as He strode under the

cold glare of the learned in the Temple court. The King whom
the chief priests failed to recognize; the Corner Stone which
the builders rejected. By that prophetic beam unlearned lips
straight from the breast forgot their infant lisping, took up a
heavenly song, a blessed revelation that thrilled the heart of
the sorrowing Lord. a fulfilment and a prophecy beyond the
wise and prudent; perfected praise upon the lips of sucklings.
"Hosanna!" they cried in the ears of marvelling mothers that
held them. "Save now, we beseech thee, Hosanna to the Son
of David!"

Who made babies seers and infants holy prophets? Who
caused the weak ones of this earth to behold the beauty of the
Lord, and the simple ones to show forth His praise? The
blessed Spirit of God with His most precious "diversities of
operations". Who could not at the gracious invitation of the
Lord earnestly covet such heavenly powers of revelation and
exultation and worship! The Lord Jesus Himself hath shed
forth this that ye now see and hear, that ye might both *see* and
hear . . .and speak, and do.

CLASSIFICATION AND DISTRIBUTION OF THE GIFTS

The verses eight to eleven quoted at the end of the last section (page 23) contain the portion that is to be dealt with in
some detail in these pages. Here we can give a simple classification of the nine Spiritual Gifts. They fall naturally into three
groups of three each. There are three Gifts of Revelation,
three of power, and three of inspiration. The third group contains the three vocal gifts.

The classification does not follow the order of the Gifts in
the passage. It will be helpful to set them out in tabular form
and give a simple definition of each.

(1) GIFTS OF REVELATION:
    (a) A Word of Wisdom. Supernatural revelation of
        divine purpose.
    (b) A Word of Knowledge. Supernatural revelation of
        facts in the divine mind.

    (c) Discerning of Spirits. Supernatural insight into the realm of spirits.

(2) GIFTS OF POWER:

    (a) Faith, Supernatural trust (passive) in God for the miraculous.

    (b) The Working of Miracles. Supernatural intervention (active) in the ordinary course of nature.

    (c) Gifts of Healing. Supernatural power to heal diseases.

(3) GIFTS OF INSPIRATION (Vocal Gifts):

    (a) Prophecy, Supernatural utterance in a known tongue.

    (b) Divers Kinds of Tongues. Supernatural utterance in an unknown tongue.

    (c) Interpretation of Tongues. Supernatural showing forth of the meaning of other tongues.

In the Scripture, as has been suggested, these three groups overflow and interlock. There are two revelation Gifts and one power Gift. Then two power Gifts and one inspiration Gift. Finally, one revelation Gift and two inspiration Gifts. From which we learn that God's infinities are not really divisible. His omnipotence is not separate from His omniscience. They are co-equal and co-active expressions of His infinity. We can isolate them, so to speak, for the purposes of analysis and examination, like the individual colours of the spectrum: but they are not separate because they are distinct. They merge and harmonize and overflow one another, and who shall say where one begins and the other ends? God's knowledge and power are really indistinguishable in His omnipresence. By the Gifts of the Spirit man gets an experience, at the will of the Spirit, of God's infinite knowledge, His infinite ability, and even His infinite presence. The swift feet of God accompanied Gehazi, for all his running, on his mercenary errand to Naaman. And in the Spirit the prophet accompanied Jehovah to the "secret place" of deception (2 Kings v, 24-26). He witnessed the interview. He saw the chariot stop. He observed the polite Syrian captain alight, heard the conversation and the bargaining. He inquires: "Whence comest thou, Gehazi? And he said, Thy servant went no whither. And he said unto him. Went not mine heart with thee, when the man turned again from his chariot to meet thee? The leprosy therefore of Naaman shall cleave unto thee, and unto thy seed for ever." There, at the disposal of the prophet, was God's knowledge, His power, and even His presence. In the Gifts of the Spirit man sees what God sees, does what God does, is where God is: "as He will."

It will be noticed that I have employed the word "supernatural" in the definition of every one of the Gifts. All the Gifts are miraculous—a hundred per cent miraculous. There is no element of the natural in them at all. They are all beyond and independent of any knowledge or ability man has or can have without them. This is what distinguishes them from the fruit of the Spirit headed by Love in Galatians v, 22 and 23. The ninefold fruit is for character. None is miraculous. The nine Gifts are for power. All are miraculous. This will appear again and again in the study of the individual Gifts.

12 For as the body is one, and hath many members, and all the members of that body, being many, are one body; so also is Christ.

13 For by one Spirit are we all baptized into one body, whether we be Jews or Gentiles, whether we be bond or free; and have been all made to drink into one Spirit.

14 For the body is not one member, but many.

15 If the foot shall say, Because I am not the hand, I am not of the body; it is therefore not of the body?

16 And if the ear shall say, Because I am not the eye, I am not of the body; is it therefore not of the body?

17 If the whole body were an eye, where were the hearing? If the whole were hearing, where were the smelling?

18 But now hath God set the members every one of them in the body, as it hath pleased him.

19 And if they were all one member, where were the body?

20 But now are they many members, yet but one body.

21 And the eye cannot say unto the hand, I have no need of thee; nor again the head to the feet, I have no need of you.

Spiritual Gifts in the possession of believers are absolutely necessary to Christ. "For as the body is one, and hath many members. . .so also is Christ" (12). They are as necessary to Him in the carrying out of His present purposes as the limbs and faculties are to the natural body. If this is not the plain meaning of this portion, embodied vitally as it is in this chapter dealing specifically with the Gifts of the Spirit, it has no meaning at all. The verses state as clearly as anything could that so far as a ministry of miraculous power is concerned, the body of Christ without the Gifts of the Spirit is a limbless trunk, blind, deaf, dumb, helpless. Or, stated in more precise terms, the members of Christ without the Gifts are as limbs bereft of vitality, paralysed, and as organs robbed of their faculties. There is little difference in power between a palsied limb and an amputated one. The Gifts in men are as divine faculties to the Lord. We are His members. The Gifts are as eyes to Him; ears, feet, lips, hands. "As He is so are we in this world" (1 John iv, 17).

When Jesus left this earth He provided that His followers (those of them who should be obedient to His command to tarry for the Spirit's enduement) should be full of power to continue undiminished and unrestricted His miraculous ministry. They were to be His lips to speak in compelling unction the words of life and miraculous deliverance; His eyes to see human need, to detect church corruptions, to know in advance coming calamity; as ears to catch a cry of distress across the miles; as hands to do in response to human appeal the mighty things He did with His own anointed hands on earth. What can this portion mean if it does not mean that the miraculous Gifts are as much a necessity to the Lord now in the members of His body, as they were in the members of His very body when He dwelt among men? Was it not the Spirit-given, Gift-accompanying anointing in the power of which He stepped into Cana's feast to turn earth's earthen cisterns into chalices for the bearing forth of heaven's wine? For is not that first of miracles a parable not only of water, but of water-pots? A parable of Pentecost as well as of the Cross?

But, say some very dear and highly esteemed Christians, the Gifts of the Spirit in any case are surely optional; you can live without them. Agreed. You can live without eyes and ears and speech. Spiritual Gifts are as optional as eyesight; you can walk without eyes, but you cannot see without them. You can be holy without Gifts, but you cannot be mighty in God without them. It is power, not holiness, that heals the sick—the power that the Gifts supply. And remember that the highest claim to holiness is weakened by an exhibition of undisguised irritation or disobedience concerning any of the commands of God. Does not holiness consist in obedience to *every* holy command of our most holy God—even the command to "desire spiritual gifts"?

There are three special reasons given by Christians to justify them in neglecting the obligation to seek Spiritual Gifts.

(1) They say everybody has them. The Gifts are somewhere unobserved in operation in the body of every Christian community! Scripture students will never be satisfied with unsupported statements. Everybody is manifestly not in possession of the Gifts, otherwise we should not be exhorted to "desire" them. And they are certainly not hidden, like secret leaven, somewhere in the church officials and workers, escaping notice and defying detection. We cannot miss a miracle! If the Gifts are there we shall have miracles for their expression. We shall not miss them; neither will our friends. Unless, of course, our friends are cynics or unbelievers. Some people can miss shining angels while their simple beasts of burden halt in reverence before them.

(2) Then there are those, as suggested above, who protest that in any case the Gifts are optional. They are not necessary and more bother than they are worth. This objection is easier to meet. If, when you have heard the voice of the Lord saying He would not have you ignorant of these Gifts; when you have heard His command to desire them, to covet them earnestly, you can still asseverate that Gifts are optional, would it be ungenerous or unreasonable to suggest it is **obedience rather** than enlightenment that is at fault?

(3) Some say that miracles finished with the apostles. One might as well say that salvation ceased with them too. There is as much Scripture ground for the one as the other. Might as well tell the lame man at the temple gate that miracles ceased with the Lord! He is too much enthralled in the enjoyment of one to engage in controversy. Might as well tell Cornelius that "tongues" ceased at Pentecost! He is too busy magnifying the Lord in other tongues to hear you. Might as well inform the Ephesians that prophecy ceased with Malachi! They are too rapt in its heavenly utterance to argue (Acts xix, 6). We are IN IT, dear critical friends! To disbelieve a present Pentecost you have got to be out of it.

All these, and many other, objections to present-day supernatural manifestations are of the class books, theological, not Scriptural. To ask the objectors to produce chapter and verse is to reduce them to impotence and confusion. And of course, the whole of our attitude to Spiritual Gifts is determined by our answer to the question, Do you or do you not believe in miracles? The man who believes in present-day miracles finds no difficulty in accepting the miracles of the Bible: he spends no time or cunning in attempting to account for them on natural grounds. You will never hear one who is familiar with miraculous operations of the Spirit casting doubt upon the Virgin birth or the divinity of the Lord Jesus. How can those who declare that miracles have ceased believe in the imminent and crowing miracle of the coming of the Lord! When the heavens are ablaze with the supernatural splendour of His presence and the saints arise in shining hosts to meet Him, will they stand aloof, incredulous, exclaiming, Impossible! Hysteria! Blasphemous! Satanic!? A whole nation missed the miracle of the incarnation through unbelief. Multitudes missed the miracle of the ascension. Will hosts of fearful and incredulous Christians miss the blazing wonder of the Parousia? Can one really believe in a sudden, cataclysmic, multitudinous, magnifical translation of the age-long dead and at the same time doubt and even scorn the sudden and miraculous healing of a fractured rib? Can we really accept without question the cosmic astonishments of Genesis and the super-miraculous rebeginnings of the Revelation, and at the same time reject the miraculous "commonplaces" of today? "Who is like unto Thee, O Lord, among the mighty ones—glorious in holiness, fearful in praises, *doing wonders?*" Has the wonder-working God of Moses and Elijah and Peter and Stephen, the God of the millennial splendours to be—has He happed upon a period of temporary helplessness in this age of desperate human need?

Verse 13 calls for some special notice in view of the frequent misinterpretation of the commentators, the pulpits and the schools.

13 For by one Spirit are we all baptized into one body, whether we be Jews or Gentiles, whether we be bond or free; and have been all made to drink into one Spirit.

For more than thirty years, ever since the commencement of this latter-day outpouring of the Holy Ghost with signs following, this verse has served as an arena for the controversialists. Over and over again it is used as a proof text for the theological contention that all believers are automatically "indwelt by the Holy Spirit" from the moment of the new birth. I am more than anxious to tread lightly and graciously upon territory that has been visited with repeated storms of irritation and even bitterness; but does not even a superficial glance at the verse in its context show that no such doctrine is hinted? The emphasis in the passage is clearly on the recurrent word "ONE" and not on the usually stressed word "all". "The body is ONE" — "by ONE Spirit" — "made to drink into ONE Spirit" — "yet but ONE body."

The thought expressed is the organic unity of the Gift-endowed members of the body of Christ. There is no question of the relationship of the "indwelling of the Spirit" to the new birth; the question is the relationship of the Gifts and the ONENESS of their divine Source. There is no question of how many Corinthians or Christians are filled with the Spirit, nor of when that infilling took place, but of how many

31

Spirits are inspiring the diverse Gifts of those who possess them – even ONE.

The lesson emphasized is that Spiritual Gifts emanating from One Source should be manifest in oneness, should produce oneness in those who possess them. The lesson is intended as a warning against schism (25) resulting from envy and competition in the use of the Gifts. As though an orator on the subject of Patriotism, speaking on London, should exhibit to his *British* audience the virtues of fraternal love and mutual loyalty, urging the same upon them by the ties of common parentage and racial relationship. The exhoration remains an excellent one even to any naturalized *Greeks* or *Jews* who may be present in the audience, but the appeal on the grounds of common parentage and consanguinity is not appropriate in their case; the fact of their naturalization, nowever, would give them an indubitable claim to identical recognition, privileges and protection with their adopted compatriots.

But what would you think of these same Greeks or Jews if, coming out of the meeting, they accosted some friends and said, "It appears that we are all of us Britishers—for the speaker has just told us that British blood is flowing in all of our veins"? No. The message of verse 13 is not that all Christians have received the Holy Ghost, but that all Christians who *have* received the Holy Ghost are filled with the *self-same* Spirit; and that fact should urge them to unity and not to schism.

Obviously, there can be no general and universal application of all Scriptures to all Christians. Would those, for instance, who claim on the basis of verse 13 that all Christians are "indwelt by the Spirit" from the moment of regeneration, also claim on the basis of verse 2 that all Christians were formerly worshippers of Bacchus and Psyche and Zeus? Is not the implication of that verse limited, not only to Corinthian Christians, but precisely to Corinthian Christians who actually *had been* worshippers of dumb idols? So also, is not verse 13 limited in its application, not only to Christians, not only to

Christians actually filled with the Spirit in contradistinction to those who were not (Acts viii, 16; xix, 2), but also to Christians filled with the Holy Spirit and actually in possession of the Gifts of the Spirit in actual operation? The whole of the confusion has arisen from the general application to Christians of Scripture statements that have a particular and really limited signification. The verse in question, considered honestly in its context, would be fairly interpreted in the following paraphrase: If we are baptized into the Spirit at all, it is into the One Spirit that we are all baptized—if we have drunk into the Spirit at all, let us remember for unity's sake that it is into the One Spirit that we have every one drunk. For those "hands" and "feet" and "eyes" that represent miraculous Gifts in the Church are all members and faculties of One Body—all Gifts of One Spirit resulting from One baptism.

COMPARISON AND HARMONY OF THE GIFTS

22. Nay, much more those members of the body, which seem to be more feeble, are necessary:

23 And those members of the body, which we think to be less honourable, upon these we bestow more abundant honour; and our uncomely parts have more abundant comeliness.

24 For our comely parts have no need; but God hath tempered the body together; having given more abundant honour to that part which lacked;

25 That there should be no schism in the body; but that the members should have the same care one for another.

26 And whether one member suffer, all the members suffer with it; or one member be honoured, all the members rejoice with it.

The thought of Unity is still the prominent one, as in the portion (12-21) considered in the last section; and the comparison of the Gifts is continued, showing a virtual equality in spite of the apparent disparity in their importance—an equality assured on the principle that what some Gifts lose in power they gain in "honour", and what some lose in frequency they gain in prominence.

THE GIFTS OF THE SPIRIT

The Spirit's design in the various Gifts is unity in diversity and harmony in seeming disparity. Harmony, indeed, perfect balance and essential interdependence, are the chief characteristics of the Gifts considered in conjunction with one another, and flawless adaptation to heavenly ends is the marvellous feature that distinguishes the individual Gifts. The analogy of the members in the human body gives a beautiful and powerful light. There is the same diversity in the Gifts as in the human members, and the same essential harmony. Some are as eyes and some as ears; some as the tongue, the hand, the nose, the foot; some even as the head, containing many faculties, representing those in possession of several Gifts. Mutual dependence is absolute as in the body, and not even the exalted Word of Wisdom can say to the humble Interpretation of Tongues, "I have no need of thee." As the feet would lose direction without the head, so the head would lack mobility without the feet. So the highest faculty stands in constant need of its remotest associate (21) and the most honourable faculty must pay constant tribute to the least. Thus do we learn also that our heavenly "Head" is incomplete without the presence of the smallest members corresponding to the "feet," and limited in His efficiency of present working by any deficiency in the Gifts, as the body is limited by the absence of even its smallest faculty. There is a part written on the orchestral score that only the triangle can supply. I like the story of the lame man and the blind man who were invited to travel some miles in difficult country to a feast. The lame man could not walk and the blind man could not see the way. Neither was able to accept the invitation until they together conceived a happy plan. They both eventually went and enjoyed the feast because the blind man carried the lame man, one lending eyes and the other feet. (Job xxix, 15). "Two are better than one," says Solomon, "because they have a good reward for their labour. For if they fall, the one will lift up his fellow."

Marvellously indeed hath God "tempered the body together." Marvellously hath He arranged for the expression of the multiple faculties of the Spirit through the diverse operations of the nine miraculous Gifts. The "best gifts" must wait attendance on the simplest as their vehicle of expression, like austere noblemen upon their liveried equerries, miracles and revelations often upon simple prophecy, and faith sometimes upon the lesser discerning of spirits. That is a quaint fable which tells how the members of the body once fell into mutiny. The stomach was the object of their revolt. Why should each member labour through the day to support an organ that lay idle, as they said, in the midst of them! The teeth would not bite another morsel for it, nor the feet carry it another inch! So they resolved and so they acted until, beginning themselves to languish, the truth was borne upon them that it was really their secret associate the stomach that lent them strength to labour and warmth to enjoy rest. "Whether one member suffer, all the members suffer with it; or one member be honoured, all the members rejoice with it". (26).

And how blessedly the Lord has assured the grand necessity of the "feeble members" (22), granting them abundant honour by generous distribution and abundant comeliness by protection and control. For Tongues and Interpretation, like fingers and toes, being among the feebler members, are the most generously distributed, and, like veins and nerves, more jealously and carefully safeguarded. The whole of a long chapter (xiv) is devoted to the regulation and protection of the feebler and more frequent Gifts of Prophecy, Tongues and Interpretation of Tongues, whereas the Spirit is content to launch the larger Gifts in a sentence, like rare orbs in the spiritual firmament, leaving them to their splendour and rarity as their chief protection and regulation.

27 Now ye are the body of Christ, and members in particular.
28 And God hath set some in the church, first apostles, secondarily prophets, thirdly teachers, after that miracles, then gifts of healings, helps, governments, diversities of tongues.
29 Are all apostles? are all prophets? are all teachers? are all workers of miracles?
30 Have all the gifts of healing? do all speak with tongues? do all interpret?
31 But covet earnestly the best gifts:

There are those who will say, quoting verse 27, that of course it is believers who are the "members' referred to in the chapter: "Ye are the members" (27). Others will say, still quoting this verse. it is believers in their several *offices* that are especially the "members" in question: "Some apostles, some prophets, some teachers" (29). But is it not true, still keeping in view the same verse and its context, that, whether plain believer or office-bearer, it is the *Gifts* that render either miraculously effective?—"Miracles, healings, tongues" (28). And is not this the clear subject of this portion where all three are significantly interwoven—plain believers, their offices and their spiritual Gifts, showing the essential inter-relationship between them. It is *hearing* that makes the ear and properly constitutes it a member of the body. Similarly it is the Gifts of the Spirit endowing the members that makes them effective members of Christ in His present supernatural ministry.

All Christians are certainly members of Christ, but for the purpose of Paul's unfolding of the Gifts in these three chapters (xii-xiv) he is still thinking in verse 27 of those members of Christ who, like the Corinthians, were positively endowed with one or other of the miraculous Spiritual Gifts. We must, in short, constantly bear in mind that Paul is dealing in these chapters with members of the Body not simply as saved but as also empowered with the miraculous equipment of the Spirit. True it is the Cross that saves and renders one a member of the heavenly family, but it is the enduement, anointing, infilling, baptism of the Holy Spirit that equips with the Gifts and renders one a miraculous member of the miracle-working body of Christ in the sense of this portion.

A sufficient comment on verse 31 to those who listen to "every word that proceedeth out of the mouth of God" will be to repeat it in italics: *But covet earnestly the best gifts.*

31. . . .and yet show I unto you a more excellent way.

Having accepted God's blessed salvation, having sought and received the fullness of His Spirit, having earnestly coveted the best Gifts, and being now in conscious possession of some "manifestation of the Spirit", we must next attend as earnestly to God's unfolding of the *best way* in which to employ this heavenly gift. But so many leaders and teachers deal with this clause as though it neutralized all the rest of the chapter. As though our all-wise God had erected a pretentious castle of insubstantial material and swept it away with an afterthought; as though He had built us a magnificent ideal in a chapter of thirty-one verses and demolished it in a final phrase.

The very various translations of scholarly commentators indicate that the rendering of our Authorized Version is not at all certain. "Yet I can still show you a way beyond all comparison the best," says the Twentieth Century New Testament. "And moreover, beyond them all, I will show you a path wherein to walk," is the rendering of Conybeare and Howson. A Greek scholar and personal friend allows that the original will easily bear the translation, "Yet I show you the way in its highest form," while Ellicott comments: "The more excellent way is not some gift to be desired to the exclusion of the other gifts, but a more excellent way of striving for those gifts. That which will consecrate every struggle for attainment and every gift when attained is LOVE."

Obviously it is unreasonable and mischievous for critical friends to treat the Gifts as though they were negligible and side-track obedient seekers on to what they look upon as the safer road of Love; to sweep away the nine mighty Gifts of the Holy Spirit with an irritable gesture in the blessed name of Love. "Follow after love, AND desire spiritual gifts," says the Scripture, which, if it means anything at all, means, Cease not to seek Spiritual Gifts until you receive them and then go on to seek love as the motive principle in their employment and regulation. The Gifts of the Spirit, like beautiful and powerful steeds, are to be harnessed to the King's chariot, and the reins put into the skilful hands of Love, the heavenly Charioteer.

We will leave the further consideration of chapter thirteen, of which this phrase is really the opening clause, to a later chapter especially devoted to it. Suffice it to say, as we pass along in our reverent inquiries to the chapters that deal specifically with the individual Gifts, that God has designed in these heavenly endowments instruments for the revelation of His will, for the building up of His Church, for the inspiration of His worshippers, for the amelioration of the distressed, for the frustration of the plans of the adversary, and for the irresistible furtherance of the glorious affairs of the glorious kingdom of His ever-glorious Son.

CHAPTER FOUR

The Word of Knowledge

... to another the word of knowledge. 1 Cor. xii, 8.

THOUGH the Lord has commanded us to covet earnestly the best Gifts He has not told us clearly which those best Gifts are. There will be no attempt here to indicate the Gifts in their order of importance. Perhaps we are intended to take the list as it stands as roughly indicating the gradation. Certainly the two Gifts that stand at the head of the list must be considered among the greatest. And no doubt the Word of Wisdom comes no whit behind the very chiefest (Prov. iv, 7). In studying the Word of Knowledge first, there is no more desire to change the God-appointed order than there would be to change the sequence in the rainbow colours by considering the orange before the red. Obviously there is a relationship between Wisdom and Knowledge. It will be convenient to consider the second first.

The Word of Knowledge is the supernatural revelation by the Holy Spirit of certain facts in the mind of God. God keeps ever before Him in the storehouse of His mind all the facts of heaven and earth. He knows every person, place and thing in existence, and He is conscious of them all at the same time. It is not that He merely recalls them: that would be Memory. It is that He has them ever before Him: that is Knowledge. The Word of Knowledge is the revelation to man by His Spirit of some detail of that All-Knowledge. The revelation, perhaps, of the existence, condition or whereabouts of some person or object or place, of the location or occasion of some event. It is not the gift of knowledge but the Word of Knowledge—more exactly a Word of Knowledge, for the

39

article (the) does not appear in the original. When you ring up your solicitor in difficulty he does not give you his knowledge over the 'phone, otherwise you would become a solicitor and never need him again; he gives you a word, a fragment of it for your temporary need.

The Word of Knowledge is not a God-sent amplification of human knowledge. It is a divinely given fragment of divine knowledge. It is not knowledge that may be acquired either by study or consecration: it is knowledge miraculously conveyed, in the same way that speaking with other tongues is utterance miraculously given. It is not the sudden or gradual discovery or accumulation of things or facts about God or man: it is a divinely granted flash of revelation concerning things which were hopelessly hidden from the senses, the mind or the faculties of men. It is not an acquisition but a gift. It is not a faculty but a revelation; the faculty is in God. It is the operation, by the Spirit, of God's faculty of Knowledge, in such a way that for a specific purpose man gets a temporary gleam of God's omniscience. It is a miracle with no admixture of the natural. In its operation man is not properly speaking an agent; he is a passive recipient. He contributes nothing; he receives all. The Word of Knowledge may be the revelation of the whereabouts or the doings of a man, the nature of his thoughts or the condition of his heart. The revelation of the place where Nathaniel prayed (if he prayed) came to the Lord by the Word of Knowledge. The revelation of his guileless heart came also by the same blessed Gift.

The Word of Knowledge is not one of the vocal Gifts. It is one of the Gifts of revelation. It is not essentially vocal at all. It may be received as a silent revelation on one's knees. It becomes vocal, of course, when the revelation it brings is shared with others. Little Samuel received his Word of Knowledge and Wisdom in silence with God, some time before he made it vocal in the presence of Eli. It would have remained just as truly a Word of Knowledge if it had never become a spoken or a written Word. But God commanded him to make vocal the secret Word he had received (I Samuel iii, 13).

From the fact that it is called a Word of Knowledge has arisen the impression that it is essentially a Gift of utterance or exposition. But a word is more than an uttered sound. It is a something apart from its spoken or written symbol. The symbol is only the vestment of the word. The sound of it is not the word, neither is the shape nor the sight of it. the word WORD here is the Greek word *Logos.* According to Young that can have the sense of "word, speech, matter or reason." A Word, therefore, is really a matter or a revelation behind the symbol that is called a Word. A Word of Knowledge is a revelation of Knowledge, or a fragment of Knowledge. It is not necessarily an utterance or a scriptum of Knowledge. When that same revelation has become an utterance of Knowledge it has really borrowed the services of the sister Gift of Prophecy, or perhaps a natural sentence or two to give it expression. In itself the Word of Knowledge is not more truly an utterance than is the Gift of Discerning of Spirits.

The most illustrious use of the same word will help as an illustration, "In the beginning was the Word *(Logos)."* The Lord is more than His Word, either spoken or written. He is the Revelation behind it. In the same way He was more than the flesh He became, though that very flesh was He. The flesh was the vestment of the Word as the spoken Word is the vestment of the Revelation. The Word, like the Lord, is a Revelation: the off-flash of the Father's effulgent All-Knowledge. A Word of Knowledge is a ray of that divine off-flash for human uses, a fragment of what God knows made known to man.

It may help if we set down here some mistaken views concerning the Gift.

(1) It is confused with natural ability, natural learning, or natural enlightenment. If it were any of these it would not be a Gift but an accomplishment. It is not natural but super-natural. The manifestations of the Spirit are beyond the sphere of the natural. Natural ability or characteristics may influence the expression of the Gift, as the tone of a voice or a foreign tongue might influence the reading of a psalm; but natural

ability is neither the source nor the agency of the revelation. The Holy Spirit is both Source and Agency. The Word of Knowledge is distinct from natural knowledge, however highly developed, for the following reasons:

(a) The Word of Knowledge is an operation of the Spirit, as when John received the revelation of the condition of the seven churches when he was in the Spirit on Patmos (Rev. i, ii, iii). Natural knowledge is the fruit of natural faculty, as when Gamaliel learned of the insurrections under Theudas and Judas of Galilee and recounted them for his friends' guidance (Acts v, 34-39). John received facts that in his position it was impossible for him to learn without the revelation of the Spirit, while Gamaliel acquired historic data that were at the disposal of any man with trained natural faculties. But, of course, so far as the canon of Scripture is concerned, John with his miracle of Knowledge, Gamaliel with his acquired natural knowledge, and and Luke with his Spirit-guided record of Gamaliel's knowledge, were equally inspired of the Spirit. (b) The Word of Knowledge is a miraculous revelation, as when Elisha knew the location of the Syrian camp. "Beware that thou pass not such a place; for thither the Syrians are come down" (2 Kings vi, 9). Natural knowledge is a furnishing of the human mind by observation, conversation, reading or reflection, as when the Benjamite came to Shiloh to inform Eli of the death of his sons, Hophni and Phinehas (I Samuel iv, 16, 17). (c) The Word of Knowledge comes as a revelation without natural effort, as when Ananias received the revelation of Saul's conversion, a revelation in detail of the street, the house, its occupier, the convert, his attitude, his thought, his need (Acts ix, 11, 12). Natural knowledge is the result of intellectual effort. (d) The Word of Knowledge depends on our fellowship with God, as when Peter received his dazzling revelation, "Thou art the Christ, the Son of the living God" (Matt. xvi, 16). Natural knowledge can be independent of fellowship with God, as in the ungodly.

(2) The Gift is confused with a profound knowledge of the

Bible and theology. One of the gracious offices of the Holy Spirit is to give light on the Word, operating on the human mind and intellect. The mind of man does not operate actively in the Word of Knowledge, but the mind of the Spirit. The human mind without effort receives an image from God's mind as a sensitive plate in a camera without effort receives an impression from without. The things that the Word of Knowledge reveals could not be known through the most diligent study of the Word or theology. It was the Spirit that conveyed to the entranced Peter the fragment of divine knowledge that three men stood at the gate awaiting him: "The Spirit said unto him, Behold, three men seek thee" (Acts x, 19).

Early commentators like Wesley and Henry and Barnes thought the two Gifts of Wisdom and Knowledge were interpretative of the Scriptures. The error arose from the supposition that they were Gifts of utterance. The Word of Wisdom was generally supposed to deal with the mysteries of the gospel and the Word of Knowledge with the explanation of types and prophecies. One beloved commentator adds that the Holy Spirit imparted the Gifts to the Church (with a capital C), meaning, of course, the clergy. But the Gifts are the Holy Spirit's endowments, not only for "ministers" but for all believers who believe for them. "The manifestation of the Spirit is given to every man." As a matter of fact, no Spiritual Gifts are necessary for preaching, teaching or evangelizing. The gifts belonging to these offices are inherent in the offices. They are not miraculous gifts in the sense of the Spiritual Gifts we are considering. A God-appointed pastor or teacher or evangelist is inconceivable apart from his God-appointed message. The Spiritual Gifts are beyond the endowments necessary for the messages of Christ's messengers, and are designed for an additional purpose. They are intended for the miraculous signs accompanying and confirming their preaching, teaching or evangelizing. The light of the Spirit upon the Word and the unction of the Spirit clothing the minister are the sufficient divine equipment for the preacher's SPEAKING ministry: the Gifts of the Spirit are for the speaker's miraculous DOING ministry, confirming the Word he has spoken (Acts i, 1; Mark vi, 30). To interpret the mighty Gifts as though they were an ordinary part of the speaker's pulpit equipment is to dissipate them like lifted mists among the commonplaces of general expository abilities and ordinary Christian graces; it is to throw back into the tide like undistinguished pebbles heaven's priceless pearls.

(3) The Word of Knowledge is erroneously associated with that very real and precious knowledge of God that is acquired by long experience of His ways and doings. But neither long experience of God Himself nor rich experience of His ways can result in a miracle of revelation. The young and inexperienced may be the recipients of mighty revelations through this Gift, while the old and experienced may receive no word at all. Eli the priest had both long knowledge of God and rich experience of His ways. Yet for him in his later years "there was no open vision." The boy Samuel, on the other hand, had neither years nor experience, for "Samuel did not yet know the Lord, neither was the word of the Lord revealed unto him," yet the Lord revealed to him in a Word of Knowledge the things He had already spoken to Eli through His prophet, and in a Word of Wisdom the whole of His purpose concerning Eli and his sons for the remaining score or more years of his life, and even beyond this, the consequences of the divine displeasure affecting the progeny of Eli for ever (1 Samuel iii, 7, 11-14).

Which brings us back to our starting point, that the knowledge that comes by the Word of Knowledge is not an acquisition but a Gift. It is supernaturally imparted from above, independent of natural senses, mental faculties, education, study, observation, years or experience. It is not a development of natural knowledge but a miracle of divine knowledge. This Knowledge will never make a scholar, and a scholar by scholarship will never attain to this Knowledge. No amount of learning or knowledge of the Word or blessed Christian experience could have told Peter that the divinely appointed emissaries of Cornelius were at the gate of his lodging in Joppa: the voice of the Spirit revealed it to him through a Word of Knowledge. "The Spirit said unto him,

Behold, three men seek thee" (Acts x, 19).

A few further examples of the use of the Gift in the Scriptures will help to make this clearer. We shall recognize in these examples not only the gracious condescension of the Lord in thus opening for men a window into the secret repository of His All-Knowledge, but in a measure we shall recognize also the divine purpose in the employment of this particular Gift.

(a) To warn a king of an enemy's plan of destruction (2 Kings vi, 9-12).

The king of Syria selected a secret encampment as the base of his military operations against Israel . He forgot that "the eyes of the Lord run to and fro through the earth, beholding the evil and the good." God gave Elisha in a miracle a revelation of the hidden encampment; Elisha communicated his information to the king of Israel; "and the king of Israel sent to the place which the man of God told him and warned him of, and saved himself there, not once nor twice"; in explication of which mystery the astounded Syrian monarch received the intelligence that "Elisha the prophet that is in Israel telleth the king of Israel the words that thou speakest in thy bedchamber." A fragment of God's Knowledge thus saved a nation.

(b) To enlighten and encourage a discouraged servant of the Lord (1 Kings xix, 14-18).

Elijah fled before the threats of the enraged Jezebel. "In wrath she hated him" for invoking heaven's fire upon her idolatrous Baalite priests. At the granite door of the cave in Horeb he poured out his exaggerated complaint before the Lord who visited him there. The corruption and apostasy of Israel is complete! — he mourned. "They have forsaken thy covenant, thrown down thine altars, and slain thy prophets with the sword; and I, even I only, am left." Then came the miracle of divine Knowledge astounding the gloom-infected prophet, "I have left me *seven thousand,* all the knees which have not bowed unto Baal!" What a comfortable Word of Knowledge for a discouraged servant whose jealousy for the Lord and consequent tremors had caused him to fear he was alone!

(c) To expose a hypocrite (2 Kings v, 20-27).

For when God opens His hand, bestowing lavish gifts upon the needy through the miracle-ministry of His servants, envy unlawfully arises to enrich itself, hindering God's work and embarrassing His servants! The miracle-light of the Spirit falls like a ray in the dark upon secret dishonesty. God's miracle-light supervises His miracle benefits, the Gifts thus proving mutually protective. "Gehazi, the servant of Elisha the man of God, said, Behold, my master spared Naaman the Syrian in not receiving at his hands that which he brought; but, as the Lord liveth, I will run after him, and take somewhat of him." God focused the mighty lens of His Knowledge, giving His faithful servant a glimpse, exposing the treachery and safeguarding His precious benefactions. Gehazi assuredly "took somewhat of" Naaman. Not his glittering silver; not his coveted Damascene raiment: his snowy leprosy.

(d) To convince a sinner of the need of a Saviour. (John iv, 18, 19, 29.)

Take away the miracle from the wellside that burning day in Sychar and the marvellous interview of the sinner and the Lord of Glory would have ended in the tiresome parry and thrust of futile controversy. "Come, see a man," said the convinced and newly saved sinner—not, "Whose manners are more elegant, whose syllables more eloquent, whose theology more impressive than any that ever I heard"; but, "Come, see a man which told me all things that ever I did"! How did Jesus learn the sinner's secret history? The Spirit He received at His baptism in Jordan enlightened Him in a Word of His Father's Knowledge.

(e) To discover a man in hiding (1 Samuel x, 22).

Where is young Saul the Benjamite, doubly confirmed in his appointment to the throne of Israel; chosen by the Spirit and already anointed; chosen by public lot, the human act confirming the divine, the natural attesting the supernatural? Where is he? Bring him forth. For all his stature and goodliness and majesty of mien he trembles, as well he might, at the thought of a throne. He has hidden himself. He cannot be found. "They inquired of the Lord if the man should yet come thither. And the Lord answered, Behold, he hath hidden himself among the stuff." A Word of God's Knowledge and every secret thing is brought to light.

(f) To indicate a man in need (Acts ix, 11).

For how could poor Saul of Tarsus have recovered his sight and strength and received his final equipment for service in the baptism of the Spirit if the Lord had not given to timid Ananias in a Word of divine Knowledge a detailed revelation of his needs?

(g) To reveal corruption in the Church (Acts, v, 3).

And is not the Church of Christ suffering today from that duplicity in certain of its members that can only be brought to light and corrected supernaturally by the Gifts of the Spirit, as in the days when the dissembling man and his wife lied to the Holy Ghost, imperilling the whole of God's plan for supplying the needs of his beloved poor? (Acts iv, 34-37).

(h) To indicate a suitable place for a meeting of God's people (Mark xiv, 13-15).

For in the same blessed way that the Spirit indicated to the Lord Jesus a suitable guest chamber for meeting with his people, in a city that would seem to contain no such place, so today the people of God may through a similar Word of Knowledge succeed in finding an assembly room for worship when every human endeavour has failed.

(i) To know men's thoughts (John ii, 24; 1 Samuel ix, 19).

"I will tell thee all that is in thine heart." Jesus knew not only "all men" but also "what was in man." How different on occasions would our actions be, and how much more effectively we should serve the Lord if, as Samuel at Ramah or Jesus at Jerusalem, we too might, by the mighty searchlight of God's Knowledge, know men's thoughts and the good or evil drift of their imaginings!

And how naturally we turn from Scripture uses of the Word of Knowledge to present-day uses of the Gift, answering in a word the critic's twofold query. Where are the Gifts, and, in any case, what is the use of them?

(A) The Word of Knowledge can mightily aid in effectual prayer either for God's servants in distress or for those in need of spiritual help.

As the result of a certain young woman's Spirit-given vision in vivid detail of three missionaries in peril, and her consequent effectual prayers in the Holy Ghost, the three missionaries in question, in a land thousands of miles away enjoyed instant deliverance.

It is recorded of Mr. W. Burton, of the Congo Evangelistic Mission, that he lay actually dying among a circle of despairing friends, when suddenly, for no human reason that anybody could discover or imagine, he rose out of a state of death into the full vigour of perfect health! The reason was not forthcoming until months later when Mr. Burton returned to England on furlough. A comparison of diary entries between him and a young woman in Preston revealed that on the very day and at the very hour when Mr. Burton was given up for dead the Spirit showed the whole scene in a revelation of God's Knowledge to the sister in question, who, instantly overcome by the Spirit's power, agonized long in an unknown tongue before God until she saw the beloved missionary get up restored in her vision!

Mr. Stanley Frodsham, our esteemed brother and Pentecostal leader across the water, tells in a biography of his late wife Alice, how that she had a young Christian friend rescued out of a sinful home, who occasionally manifested distressful leanings towards the old life of the world. One day the Spirit gave Mrs. Frodsham in a Word of Knowledge a revelation of the youth's danger. She saw him on his way to his old haunts. She saw him stop, arrested by the Spirit. She saw him join an open-air meeting. She prayed for him until she beheld the Spirit of God prevail in the youth's reclamation. With what astonishment he listened to a detailed recital of his day's experiences from the lips of his friend when he saw her in the evening!

(B) To recover lost persons or property.

As in the case of young Saul recounted above, God can serve His people today by placing His heavenly spotlight upon things and people that have got out of the range of our vision or knowledge. Like the young man who lost his cherished fountain pen and discovered it in the exact place under an oak tree in a particular field the Lord showed his father in a vision while at prayer.

And should there be those who read that exclaim, "What a trifling use to ascribe to God's great Gifts," let them pause and ask themselves if a miracle can ever be a trifle, or if on the other hand the most "trifling" demonstration of God's supernatural powers can ever be less than a miracle. There would be those no doubt (if they could have seen him), beholding Elijah taking his morning meal by Cherith, who would exclaim, "Only bread, after all!" But let it be remembered that every tiny beakful of such common bread calls for the inconceivable almightiness of our miracle-working God!

(C) To reveal facts in private lives for spiritual correction or profit.

This is the story as that admirable man of God, F.B. Meyer, tells it:

"I remember speaking in the Free Assembly Hall at Edinburgh, and as I was standing on the platform there in the evening I noticed a young man come into the gallery, a student, as I thought. He sat intently watching me and listening. During my address I happened to say—but why I said it I have no idea—"There is a man here who owes his employer £3.90p, and unless that is repaid he will never get peace with God." On the great staircase Professor Simpson, with whom I was staying, said to this young man, to my great surprise: 'Will you take luncheon with Mr. Meyer tomorrow?' He said, 'I shall be very pleased.'

"We sat together at the luncheon table and talked on indifferent matters. He said to me: 'Are you going again to the Assembly Hall this afternoon?' I said, 'Certainly.' He said, 'May I walk with you?' and as soon as I got outside he took my arm convulsively in his and said: 'You know me!' 'No,' I said, 'I have never seen you except last night when you came into the gallery.' 'The remarkable thing is,' he said, 'that three years ago I took just £3.90p from my employers, I am a Christian man; it has been on my heart ever since, but I didn't like the exposure of returning it. But here is a letter to them, and you will see the cheque inside for just the amount.' I read the letter, replaced the cheque, posted it, and as that letter passed into the pillar box, his soul rose up in a perfect hundredth psalm of thanksgiving."

Since the third edition of this book was printed I have been in Canada and America for five years' ministry, mostly on the Gifts and the supernatural, and have there observed many astonishing examples of the operation of this gift of a Word of Knowledge. I have therefore broken into this latest edition to give examples that have come under my own observation in the ministry of two evangelists in whose meetings I have taken humble part. There is room only for the briefest statement of these fully documented accounts.

In Arkansas, in a meeting where I just briefly testified, the evangelist suddenly stopped in his ministering to the sick. Turning to the great audience and pointing out a young man, he said: "Young man, the Lord tells me you are living in sin. You are not only smoking, but drinking heavily. Moreover, the Lord gave you a call to the ministry long ago and you ignored it. Again, you are suffering from T.B. in an advanced state of development, and you are wondering how you can be healed. Is that right?"

"Yes, sir," came the prompt reply.

"Then come out now and the Lord will restore and heal you." He came out, and was by his changed appearance obviously both restored and healed. Who told the evangelist these secret facts in the man's life? Of course God did. How? Through this blessed gift of a Word of Knowledge. God knew those facts, and there and then in a flash of revelation made known to His servant these elements of His supernatural knowledge. In the same meeting the evangelist turned to a sister who had come for healing, and after telling her (without looking at her "healing card") she was suffering from nervous fears and exhausation, said, "I see you standing at a window this time yesterday afternoon. You were weeping. You had a cloth over your arm as if you had been washing up the pots. You were weeping, wondering how you could get into this meeting to be healed. Is that right?"

"Yes," was the reply.

Who told the evangelist these intimate details in the private life of an unknown woman? God. By this same mighty gift of a Word of Knowledge.

Take another evangelist whom I knew personally. He told a story of how God revealed information through this gift.

"I had an unsaved sister who was sick in Los Angeles, California. I dreamed one night that instead of my sister Mary being sick in Los Angeles she was dying in Sapulpa, Oklahoma. It seemed as if she were in bed with a white sheet over her head, and on this sheet in orange letters were the words, *'No smoking.'* The room filled with light. It made me afraid. All of a sudden I could hear my sister say, 'I'm healed! I'm saved!' The white light vanished and I could see her running back and forth, praising God. I awoke. The dream stayed with me. One morning I received a telegram saying that my sister Mary was dying in *Sapulpa, Oklahoma.* She had double pneumonia and was given up to die. I rushed to the airport just in time to catch the plane to San Antonio. From there I took the bus to Sapulpa. I phoned the Sapulpa hospital and asked them if my sister Lucille were there. They replied, 'Yes, she is here,' and they called her to the phone. I asked her, 'Lucille, how is Mary?' She answered, 'She's just waiting for you to get here, to die. The doctors have given her up.' I ran for a taxicab and said to the driver, 'Take me to Sapulpa, Oklahoma as fast as you can.' We arrived. I jumped out of the cab and ran up the hospital steps. All my relatives were standing there. I hurried into the room where Mary was, took her hand and began to pray. There she lay unconscious under an oxygen tent; it was white, with the words written on it in *orange letters, 'No Smoking.'* This was my dream! I prayed to God. He said, 'Tell everyone you see that I am going to heal your sister.' About four o'clock that afternoon Mary awoke from her coma and said, 'Mama, I'm so hungry. Won't you get me something to eat?' The doctor said they might give her any thing she desired. She was dying in any case. 'What do you want?' asked her mother. 'I want some bacon, eggs, toast and coffee!' She ate it ravenously. Ten minutes later the doctor examined her. 'This is a miracle,' he said. 'The air is breaking under those lungs that have been packed full of pneumonia!' Mary went to sleep. The doctor asked if she had vomited what she had eaten. 'No.' More amazement! Mary slept till eight o'clock that night. She awoke and said, 'Mama, I'm so hungry. Do get me something to eat.' Mother phoned an inquiry to the doctor. He asked, 'Has she vomited the other yet?' 'No.' He came and examined her and then with tears rolling down his cheeks, looked up and said, 'These lungs are absolutely clear. Her heart is beating normally. Her pulse is normal. There is no reason for this woman to be in bed. Something has happened!' My sister was saved and was home in a few days, sweeping floors, and singing, praising and magnifying God."

Someone might ask who showed the evangelist the white sheet with the orange letters. God did, by the Word of His Knowledge. Who led him, not to Los Angeles, but to Oklahoma? God, by a combination revelation of His Knowledge and Wisdom.

I have witnessed scores of revelations of this sort in this latest revival in U.S.A. There can be no reasonable doubt that these instances are examples of the operation of a Word of Knowledge. What God knows He thus makes known to His servants as He will. These are not examples of what is mistakenly called "the gift of 'Discernment'." There is, as we shall see when we come to it in these studies, no such gift as that which is loosely called "Discernment." That gift is precisely "Discerning of *Spirits*," and is limited in its operation to the realm of spirits, showing the character of spirit operating during miraculous manifestations. Neither can these above manifestations be revelations through the Gift of Prophecy. This will be clear when we arrive at that gift in our studies. The limitations of Prophecy are clearly seen in 1 Corinthians xiv, 3—"edification, exhortation, comfort." The fact that an Old Testament prophet was sometimes called a "seer" has caused some to suppose that as "seers" the "prophets" received such revelations. But of course the prophets did not receive such "seers'" revelations through their gift of Prophecy, but through an additional gift of a Word of Knowledge—a gift which anybody, prophet or no prophet may operate as God will. This later gift constituted the "prophets", "seers."

Here another matter concerning these Divine Healing campaigns may be mentioned. The revelation of the disorder the seeker is suffering from is sometimes thoughtlessly referred to as "diagnosis." This is obviously a mistake. Diagnosis is a natural deduction from symptoms. But the spontaneous announcement of a particular disease the seeker is suffering from is a revelation by the Spirit through the Gift of a Word of Knowledge.

Space prevents further examples of the present-day uses of this mighty Gift. Every purpose the Gift has served in the Scripture record, allowing for the difference in modern conditions, it will equally serve today.

As we pass to the consideration of the sister Gift of the Word of Wisdom, we may say, as a guide to the identification of this Gift in operation, that the revelation the Word of Knowledge brings is never future. Distance makes no difference to its operation. Age, education, nationality make no difference to its reception. Through its agency the whole realm of facts is at the disposal of the believer as the Spirit wills. Through its beneficent agency the Church may be purified, the distressed comforted, the saint gladdened, lost property rediscovered, the enemy defeated and the Lord Jesus glorified in all.

CHAPTER FIVE

The Word of Wisdom

. . . to one is given by the Spirit the word of wisdom. 1 Cor. xii, 8

THE Word of Wisdom is the first, the chief, no doubt of the mighty miracle-administrations of the Holy Ghost the Only-Wise God, the King Eternal.

It has already been agreed that wisdom and knowledge are related. Natural wisdom, the dictionary tells us, is the ability to apply possessed knowledge and experience. The relationship between supernatural Wisdom and supernatural Knowledge is roughly the same as between natural wisdom and natural knowledge. But of course supernatural Wisdom and Knowledge exist on a plane infinitely above their natural and human counterparts. They are God's Wisdom and Knowledge and not man's at all. That is to say that just as natural wisdom is natural knowledge naturally and humanly applied, so supernatural Wisdom is supernatural Knowledge supernaturally and divinely applied. Though the Word of Wisdom and the Word of Knowledge are definitely related to one another, the Word of Wisdom has no more relationship to natural wisdom than the Word of Knowledge has to natural knowledge, as we found in the last chapter. Supernatural Wisdom is not natural wisdom developed, augmented or intensified.

It was said in the last chapter also that God keeps ever before Him in the storehouse of His infinite mind all the facts of heaven and earth. That circumstance constitutes His infinite Knowledge. But we must add that He also keeps before Him in the same divine storehouse all the facts of time and eternity: not only all the facts that are and that have been, but all the facts that shall be throughout the eternal ages. That circumstance, we shall see, constitutes His infinite Wisdom.

For since God is ever conscious of all present things and all future things, He must also be ever conscious of that infinite gradation of things that lie between present and far future, those happenings that actually translate the present into the future. This constant development of God's known present into God's known future is really the expression of His sovereign Purpose, His determinate Counsel, His Applied Knowledge and Experience, His Wisdom. So that the moment God shows a man a glimpse of some event that has not yet transpired He has really given him a fragmentary revelation of His infinite Purpose; He has virtually shown him what He is going to do between now and then and His reason for doing it; He has given him a Word of His divine Wisdom.

Like those chess problems we sometimes see in the papers, with diagram of a board and men in position, and the challenge, "White to move and mate in five." Now if the White player shows us the board (as an expert can) as it will appear at the position of checkmate five moves ahead, he has really shown us not only the end, but his means toward that end, his plan, his irresistible purpose. That is, his knowledge of the present position added to his knowledge of the future position really constitutes his wisdom, that intelligent planning which inexorably enforces every future position. The king is checked inextricably by the expert White player virtually before he makes his first move. So with God. His consciousness of past and present is His Knowledge. His consciousness of the future is of course His Foreknowledge. His power to enforce that future is His Determinate Counsel. His intelligent Plan employing His infinite Knowledge thus becomes His irresistible Will, His Design, His Purpose, His Wisdom.

Exchange the puppet king in the illustration above for a real king, even evil-hearted Ahab, and behold the ineffable Jehovah administering move by move His inextricable "check" upon the king, and at the same time communicating His plan to His servant Elijah in a Word of His astonishing Wisdom.

Here is the board in position as the divine Checkmater saw it in the *present* and revealed it in a Word of Knowledge to

Elijah: "Arise, go down to meet Ahab king of Israel. . . .he is in the vineyard of Naboth, whither he is gone to possess it." (1 Kings xxi, 18). Here is the position as the divine Disposer *foresaw* it a year or two ahead: "And a certain man drew a bow at a venture. . . .So the king died. . . .and the dogs licked up his blood; and they washed his armour; according unto the word of the Lord which He spake" (1 Kings xxii, 34-38). And, to travel backwards over events, here is that same word of the Lord which He spake two years before, the Word of Wisdom that He gave to Elijah apprising him of His future Purpose concerning the evil king, who dared to receive the murderous spoil at the hands of his execrable queen: "Thou shalt speak unto him, saying, Thus saith thè Lord, Hast thou killed, and also taken possession?. . . .In the place where dogs licked the blood of Naboth shall dogs lick thy blood, even thine" (1 Kings xxi, 19). In those three Scriptures is seen the development of God's inexorable Purpose and the communication of a fragment of it to man in a Word of Wisdom.

The Word of Wisdom is therefore the supernatural revelation, by the Spirit, of Divine Purpose; the supernatural declaration of the Mind and Will of God; the supernatural unfolding of His Plans and Purposes concerning things, places, people: individuals, communities, nations. And since this divine Purpose is expressed to men in the exhibition of positions as they will exist in the future, that Purpose must also be expressed in the giving of those divine commands and instructions which make for the development of those future positions. In a word, the Word of Wisdom is expressed not only in foretelling future events, but in those commands and instructions which God gives men, arising out of His knowledge of those future events. It was through this Gift that Moses received the Ten Commandments, those *general* laws containing the universal requirements of God; also the ceremonial ordinances of Leviticus, containing His *particular* requirements in His ancient people. It was also a Word of Wisdom that conveyed His specific instructions concerning individuals, as when He commanded Elijah to anoint Hazael and Jehu and Elisha, or as when He gave Jonah his eight-word fiat to Nineveh, a message which was at once a prophecy, a threat and an exhortation. The Word of Wisdom may thus be manifested through the audible divine Voice. It may also be manifested by angelic visitation, by dream or vision, or through the spiritual Gifts of Prophecy, or Tongues and Interpretation.

The Word of Wisdom is distinct from the Word of Knowledge, though they are closely related, and often as subtly intergraded in their manifestation as the rainbow colours. The Word of Knowledge is the revelation of *past* happenings or of things existing or events taking place in the *present.* The Word of Wisdom is the revelation of the Purpose of God concerning people, things or events in the *future* or looking to the future. By the Word of Knowledge John on Patmos knew the *condition* of the seven churches: by the Word of Wisdom he was able to give them the *mind, will,* and *commands* of God.

All that was said in the definition of the Word of Knowledge concerning its supernatural character must be repeated of the Word of Wisdom. It is not a development of the God-endowed faculty of human natural wisdom. It is the expression of divine faculty. Only God's faculty of Wisdom could convey such future facts and indicate such future plans as Jehoshaphat received concerning the invasion of Moab as recorded in 2 Chronicles xx, 16, 17.

It will be helpful, as in the former chapter, to glance at a few of the mistaken views concerning the Gift.

(a) It is confused with a high degree of intellectual or moral efficiency, as displayed, for instance, by the Anglican bishops in their recent task of overhauling their Prayer Book. With every desire to respect those estimable men it must be said that, however spiritual may have been their aim or helpful the result, such work is entirely the product of human effort. The task was a self-imposed task and their book is a humanly devised book. Their human efforts may or may not have been sanctified efforts. They may or may not have been aided in their human efforts by the Spirit of God. But their work was certainly not an example of the operation of this supernatural Gift of the Word of Wisdom. Albeit it is claimed as such in ecclesiastical quarters. Similar claims are of course made for the rubrics and breviaries of Romanism; claims that are summarily set aside by Anglican theologians. Or can the Modernist bodies claim an operation of this or any blessed Gift of the Holy Spirit, or even any degree of divine aid at all, in the preparation, say, of a new Hymn Book that expunges fundamental Atonement hymns and multiplies hymns that encourage unscriptural self-righteousness? Yet such a claim is undoubtedly made in Modernistic circles.

The Gifts of the Spirit are not to dictate the terms of hymns or prayers or to aid in ecclesiastical refinements. The Word of God and sanctified intelligence are sufficient for these things. A Word of Wisdom is a miracle. A supernatural operation of God's Faculty of Wisdom. It was not Paul's wisdom, though he was a wise man, that told him the details of the Coming of the Lord as recorded in 1 Thessalonians iv, 16; nor was it his mighty knowledge of the Scriptures; it was a Word of Wisdom. Natural ability, intellectual efficiency, moral quality, do not operate in the Word of Wisdom.

(b) The Word of Wisdom is confused with deep spiritual insight and unusual understanding of the more mystical parts of God's Word or the sublimities of the gospel.

As has been said before, believers may have revelation on the Scriptures without possessing any of the Gifts of the Spirit, or even without receiving the Baptism in the Spirit. The Gift is not for the unfolding of God's revealed will *in* His Word, but for the unfolding of His unrevealed will, and the declaration of His hidden purposes, *apart* from His Word. It is not a gift of utterance but of revelation. It is not a gift of exegesis. Utterance may be divine. So may be exegesis. But they are not of the Nine Supernatural Gifts. Matthew Henry's gift as an expositor was not the Gift of Wisdom or of Knowledge. It was a gift of teaching involved in his office as a

"Teacher" (Eph. iv, 11).

The Gifts are not for Bishops and Doctors of Divinity and "Reverends." They are for believers; degreed or not degreed; ordained or not ordained: artisans, warehousemen, tradesmen, labourers, housemaids, charwomen, peasants, fisherman, carpenters, you, me.

(c) It is confused with administrative wisdom, say, such as is found in the President of the Methodist Conference. But such wisdom is regularly found in the cultured natural mind, the same wisdom (sanctified, if you will) that runs a successful business or institution in the world. The ability to govern in divine things is a special supernatural endowment quite apart from any of these nine Gifts of the Spirit, and even independent of natural gifts: "Governments" (1 Cor. xii, 28). The blessed Carpenter of old by supernatural endowment made a better fisherman than the experts Peter and John. The beloved tentmaker by the same supernatural gifts made a better mariner than the governor of the vessel upon which he was a prisoner. So Peter the fisherman made a better spiritual organizer than the learned priests and scribes.

(d) It is confused with divine wisdom.

Supernatural Wisdom is divine, but not all divine wisdom is supernatural. "The fear of the Lord is the beginning of wisdom." But that wisdom is not the supernatural Gift, producing literal miracles.

The comparison in 1 Corinthians i, ii and iii is not between natural wisdom and supernatural wisdom, but between human wisdom and divine wisdom. Between "man's wisdom" and "the wisdom of God" (I Cor. ii, 4, 7). Divine wisdom is not associated necessarily with human wisdom, but likelier with human "foolishness" (1 Cor. i, 21). That is the argument of these chapters. The gift of "foolishness" rather than the gift of "wisdom" is associated with divine wisdom. That is, God does not meet the world's wisdom with a larger measure of the same order (1 Cor. i, 27): He meets it with divine wisdom, which has all the appearance of foolishness to men. This divine Wisdom Christ Jesus is "made unto us." But this is not the divine Miracle-Wisdom of the Word of Wisdom. It has no more, indeed, of the literal miraculous about it than Righteousness or Sanctification or Redemption, those other blessed phases of divinity which Christ Jesus is equally "made unto us" (1 Cor, 1, 30). The Word of Wisdom is not only divine, that is, opposed to human wisdom: it is also supernatural, miraculous, that is, opposed to natural, non-miraculous wisdom. The wisdom in 1 Corinthians ii, 6, 7, is the wisdom of the gospel conveyed under divine inspiration. The Word of Wisdom is a glance, so to speak, into the hidden realm of God's future plans and purposes.

(e) It is confused with "wiseness" or prudence or discretion or sagacity in word or act. That wisdom, for instance, which originates the Proverbs or lives by them. Take Proverbs x, 4. "The hand of the diligent maketh rich." That is not supernatural wisdom. It is natural wisdom divinely inspired, divinely authorized and divinely recorded. It is inspired and sanctified "common sense." Many godless nations have such wise sayings, and many godly men quite apart from the Bible have written such. In their case it is wisdom inspired only by the human spirit, a force which is by no means inactive either in the sanctified or the unsaved. "Why even of yourselves judge ye not what is right?" said the Lord Jesus. Natural wisdom is divinely authorized but it is the reverse of supernatural. It is God's Spirit and God's Faculty that are operative in the Word of Wisdom. "Wiseness" may or may not be divine. A Word of Wisdom is both divine and miraculous. The "wisdom" that James says we are to ask of God is general wisdom in the things of God. Solomon's wisdom was a divine increase of natural wisdom, sanctified, as the classic instance of it recorded by the Holy Ghost will show (1 Kings iii, 16). A Word of Wisdom (or rather, Knowledge) would have shown him without experiment the mother of the child. His divinely given natural wisdom conceived the plan of dividing the living child. It was a *faculty* of wisdom Solomon received of the

Lord. "I have given thee a wise and an understanding heart." That wisdom was no more supernatural than the riches that God gave him at the same time. The Word of Wisdom as interpreted by the commentators is only a degree of *human* wisdom. The Wisdom of the Spiritual Gift is an expression of the *divine* Faculty, a flash of the rotary-light of God's Wisdom in the pitchy darkness of natural wisdom.

Some Scripture examples of the use of the Word of Wisdom will show how indispensable is this Gift to poor ignorant and helpless mortals such as the best of us are.

(1) To warn and guide people concerning future judgment or peril.

"And God said unto Noah, The end of all flesh is come before me. . . .I will destroy them. . . .Make thee an ark" (Gen. vi, 13-22). God's knowledge of a future peril communicated without intermediary to man, with His purposes and helping instructions. Thus "Noah was warned of God of things not seen as yet."

"And the men said unto Lot, Hast thou here any besides? Bring them out. . . .for we will destroy this place" (Gen. xix, 12, 13). A Word of Wisdom by the voice of angels.

"And being warned of God in a dream that they should not return to Herod, they departed into their own country another way" (Matt. ii, 20). A Word of Wisdom to the ignorantly Wise in a supernatural dream. Deliverance out of danger was the end in each of these instances. Has God left us at the mercy of such perils in this Day of Grace?

(2) To reveal God's plans to those He is going to use.

"And Joseph answered Pharaoh, It is not in me: God shall give Pharaoh an answer. . . .What God is about to do He showeth unto Pharaoh. . . .Famine. . . .look out a man discreet and wise. . . .lay up corn. And Pharaoh said, Can we find such a one. . . .in whom the Spirit of God is? See, I have set thee over all the land of Egypt" (Gen. xli, 16, 28-41). A Word of Wisdom to appoint a leader, save a people and institute a dispensation.

(3) To assure a servant of God of his divine commission.

61

Forty years forsaken (?) in the Midian desert. Eighty years old. How shall Moses know he must yet deliver his brethren? A theophany on his daily round. A shekinah-illumined bush. The Voice of God. "Come now therefore, and I will send thee unto Pharaoh, that thou mayest bring forth my people out of Egypt." Would not such a Word enhearten God's tried leaders in the making today?

Down the centuries. A man in the dust beside his affrighted steed. A dazzling Splendour beyond the glory of the Eastern sun. A Voice. The same that urged the aged shepherd into the audience chamber of the supercilious Pharaoh. "Rise, and stand upon thy feet: for I have appeared unto thee for this purpose, to make thee a minister . . ." (Acts xxvi, 16). Would that God's ministers today were commissioned by such a mighty Word of His Wisdom.

(4) To reveal the acceptable order and manner of divine worship.

For how shall God's numerous people, now grown into a nation, lately come from idolatrous influences in Egypt, with no written Word for guide—how shall they know in what way Jehovah may be approached in His awful Holiness by the sin-stained children of men? The whole mighty scheme of redemption in detail in an object lesson Moses receives in the flaming Mount. The Tabernacle with its blood-stained way unto the Presence in the glory-lighted sanctuary of skins, in the wilderness trodden by the alien. "And look that thou make all after the pattern shown thee in the mount" (Exodus xxv). That tremendous Word of Wisdom decoded and traced out by obedient feet today will lead the poor sinner past Calvary's blood-soaked Altar into the dazzling precincts of the eternal Throne.

(5) To unfold to a prejudiced sectarian God's universal offers of grace.

How can a fanatical Judaist, with a selfish "unction" of strict legalism oozing from every pore, be convinced of the glorious truth that Jehovah loves godless Gentiles, and died for even them? Supernatural hunger. A Holy Ghost anointing that prostrated him. A vision. Heaven open. Food for the hungry from the divine larder. Flesh, clean and unclean! "Rise. . . .eat." The thunders of Leviticus! Religious prejudice. Rebellion. Repeated vision and Voice. "What God hath cleansed, that call not thou common!" (Acts x, 9-16). A Word of Wisdom, shattering the barrier whose foundations were built of Sinai's granite; opening a Gospel Door unto the outcast Gentiles. Hallelujah!

(6) To assure of coming deliverance in the midst of calamity.

A tempestuous wind in the Adriatic. A helpless ship mercilessly driven before it and exceedingly tossed. No sun by day: no star by night. Exhausted mariners. Bursting planks and splintering masts. All hope gone. A shining Pilot from the Port of Glory! "Fear not, Paul; thou must be brought before Caesar." Security in calamity. Heavenly Word of Wisdom like a balm-scented breeze to blow the Gospel Ship to the shores of Italy, Spain, Gaul, Britain, Home! Fear not, storm-tossed Christian. In the teeth of the furies of hell, thou too must be safely brought into the Palace of the Sovereign Lord thy Redeemer.

(7) To reveal the Will of God in all His commands and ordinances.

For every "Thou shalt" or "Thou shalt not" is really a gracious unfolding of eternal Purpose, a prophecy of felicity, a winged chariot to bear us whither the Lord would.

(8) To declare God's future acts and providences and His eternal mysteries.

How unamazed we find ourselves in the presence of the astonishing mysteries of the Word! How can we learn the secret things that belong to the Lord? Only by luminous Words of divine Wisdom that shine like planets in the dark night of our helpless ignorance. "By revelation," says Paul, "He made known unto me the mystery"—of the Gentiles' inclusion in the Church. By revelation he can confidently announce, "Behold, I show you a mystery"—concerning the sleeping and living saints at the Coming of the Lord. By revelation John sets forth in astounding focus the scene in heaven when the "rest of the dead" stand before the awful Judge on His glistering Throne. By revelation Paul foresees "the end" and the final supremacy of the Father in the Kingdom of His Son.

(9) To give assurance of blessing to come.

Surely the sun had set for ever upon unhappy Jacob that stony night in Haran had not the angels of God ascending shown him his fathers' God a constant Presence; had not the Visible Jehovah assured him in a supernatural Word, "The land whereon thou liest, to thee will I give it and to thy seed. . . .I will not leave thee until I have done that which I have spoken to thee of" (Gen. xxiii, 10-15). The same Jehovah who three hundred years before had in idolatrous Chaldea in a similar Word of Wisdom given young Abram a similar assurance (Gen. xii, 1-7).

And once again it is an easy transition from Scripture to present-day uses of the Gift. The list must be short, though it might be extended almost indefinitely. For apart from those distinguished uses of the Gift which were exclusively contributory to the Scripture canon, the uses are the same in every age till that which is perfect is come.

(A) The Word of Wisdom may be employed to warn an individual of approaching danger and to deliver from harm.

It was in those terrible days in Ireland when to be out on the streets after curfew was to invite the flying bullets and the flashing knives of the lawless. In a little kitchen bakery run single-handed by a lonely old woman of God. She told me the story herself in the bread-scented little living room with the teacakes cooling on the dresser.

"I was counting my week's takings on a Friday afternoon," she said, "—a matter of perhaps twelve pounds. Sitting on that chair, I was. A voice plainly said, 'Put that money away!'

"I looked round. Nobody in the room. I stepped to the door. Nobody in the street. I went on counting and making up my little book.

"The voice again, louder. 'Put that money away!' I looked

64

round again. No person near. 'Yes, Lord,' I said, recognizing His warning Voice, 'I am just finishing now.'

"Then louder than ever, 'Put that money away!'

"I got afraid and pushed the money quickly under a cushion on that couch, when immediately two roughs came in at the door.

" 'Hullo, Auntie!' said one; 'We have come to see you.' 'You are not my nephews,' I said.

"Then one took me by the throat and, pressing me back into a chair, put a pistol to my forehead, saying, 'Where is your money?' The other man was searching all the drawers in the room.

" 'I am a child of God,' I said, 'and that pistol will never go off!'

"Then the Spirit of the Lord got hold of me and I shouted, 'In the Name of the Lord Jesus I command you to leave this house!'

"Without another word they both took to their heels and I have never seen or heard of them from that day to this. What a blessing I didn't put the money in the drawer! Whoever would have thought of looking for money under a cushion on that old couch! Praise the Lord!"

God sees all the danger ahead of us. His gracious commands are a fragmentary unfolding of His purpose for our deliverance. Our only hope of entering into His perfect plan is in obedience to His Voice.

(B) To make known or confirm a missionary call.

A young woman in Wales received a missionary call from the Lord. How should she know the precise field of her future labours? She waited on the Lord in prayer. In vision she boarded a great ship and arrived at a strange port. Unaccustomed houses all of one sort: flat-topped. A great company of little children ran to her and clung to her arms and clothing. As they lifted their heads she saw under their conical hats yellow faces and almond eyes. China! A few years later she landed on the shores of the Orient and saw the exact houses of her vision and the same group of little children clinging to her arms and garments.

(C) To apprise of blessing or judgment to come.

Brother G., a Pentecostal leader in Ireland, was asked by a man in his congregation if he might have an opportunity of addressing the meeting. Permission was granted. While he was speaking the Lord showed the leader that this man was living in sin. The Spirit came upon him. He prophesied that unless the speaker repented he should be mocked through the streets of Belfast. He did not repent. His sin was discovered. He became the gazing stock of the whole community, being literally mocked by little children through the streets of the city.

On another occasion in a testimony meeting a stranger arose to give his testimony. It was a lying testimony. For the leader stood and spoke by the Spirit that unless the stranger repented—within three weeks he should lie dead. He did not repent. Within three weeks of that date he was killed by a bullet in the great war.

To take the brighter side, it was in a Word of Wisdom that Mr. Howard Carter received from the Lord the promise of "heaps upon heaps" of money. In the course of a few years Mr. Carter has received without special appeal many thousands of pounds for his work centring in the Bible School at Hampstead.

And to return to the serious side. A young leader in a Lancashire assembly had an engaged couple attending his meetings. Eventually the young woman accepted salvation and was filled at once with the Holy Spirit with the supernatural sign of speaking in other tongues. Her fiance, however, resisted every offer of grace and every loving appeal from his converted fiancee and the pastor of the assembly. The young woman felt obliged to break off the engagement. The man was furious. He came regularly to the meetings demanding her return and deliberately wrecked the services. One evening he was present disturbing the peace when a visiting evangelist preached the terrible judgments of God with such energy (knowing nothing, however, of the circumstances) that when he had concluded the leader felt inclined to follow with a message of peace. To his amazement, however, he found himself preaching divine judgment and warning with even greater emphasis than his young friend. The disturber of the peace heeded not. In a day or two he sickened, and in spite of desperate efforts to restore him, he died. Not the sermons, but the Purpose of God in the urgency of repeated warning was the Word of Wisdom—a rejected Word—on this occasion.

(D) To reveal the future.

Examples here are too numerous to be included. For every telling-beforehand of events to come is an operation of this blessed Gift. And every man of whom it can be said, as of Samuel, "All that he saith cometh surely to pass" (1 Samuel ix, 6) is in possession of the Word of Wisdom. The secret is as of old that the Lord tells His servants "in the ear the day before" what He knows and is about to do (1 Samuel ix, 15). And could there possibly be a more unmistakable example of the use of this Gift than the future plans that Samuel revealed to Saul when he said, "Stand still that I may show thee the word of God" (1 Samuel ix, 27)? This showing of "the word of God" was neither an introduction to the Scriptures nor an exposition of them. The context makes that clear, for Samuel proceeds, "Is it not because the Lord hath anointed thee to be captain over His inheritance?" The "word" was a revelation of the Will and Purpose of God for His chosen king. It was a Word of Wisdom.

(E) To give personal guidance in a particular direction in *special* circumstances—not to supplement human judgment in ordinary circumstances.

If an innocent child of God is brought before the courts, for instance, the Spirit may help with a positive and supernatural defence without forethought or preparation of the defendant's part. In ordinary positions, however, the Word of God is the sufficient guide in human action.

A Word of Wisdom my be expressed by illustrative action, as Agabus indicating Paul's arrest and imprisonment in Jerusalem by taking up his girdle and binding it imitatively

67

around his own limbs (Acts xxi, 11).

The expression of the Gift may vary in accordance with the office or even the personality of the one through whom it is given, as the Spirit will. Daniel the statesman receives revelation of state affairs, while Ezekiel the priest receives matters concerning the restoration of Israel. Yet since the information received is independent of natural faculties—the secret is not revealed to a man for any wisdom that he has more than any living (Daniel ii, 30)—it may be received by an inexperienced child like Samuel, an imprisoned slave like Joseph, or an exalted statesman like Daniel.

It is an axiom that every supernatural happening in the Bible or out of it, except of course counterfeit miracles of satanic origin, must be included in the sweep of the Nine Supernatural Gifts. If our chapters four and five do not convey the meaning of these Gifts of a Word of Wisdom and a Word of Knowledge, then there is a whole series of miraculous phenomena in the Bible that are not accounted for at all in the range of the Gifts of the Spirit, and we should be obliged to seek for a tenth and eleventh Gift to cover their manifestation.

To treat these mighty Gifts as vocal gifts, and suggest they are at work unobserved in preaching and teaching in the churches, is to rob them entirely of their supernatural and miraculous character. It is to strip the royal habitation of the precious treasures. To speed the robber Shishak in his felonious work. To applaud the helpless Rehoboam in his feeble remonstrance. It is to replace the golden shields of the King's House by inglorious imitations of common brass (1 Kings xiv, 25-27).

CHAPTER SIX

Discerning of Spirits

. . . .to another discerning of spirits. 1 Cor. xii, 10.

This Gift completes the cycle of the Revelation Gifts of the Spirit. Everything within the realm of Knowing—facts, events, purposes, motive, origin, destiny—human or divine or devilish, natural or supernatural, past, present or future, comes within the focal range of one or other of the three Gifts, Word of Wisdom, Word of Knowledge, or Discerning of Spirits. They include in their comprehensive survey all that God knows, and there is nothing that God knows that may not be made known to man as the Spirit wills through the agency of one or more of these three Gifts.

Discerning of Spirits possesses a much more limited range than the other two. Its powers of revelation are restricted to a single class of objects, like the great telescope that is synchronized in its movements to the revolution of a single planet and its system.

The Gift is entirely supernatural, just as speaking with other tongues is supernatural. It differs from the Word of Wisdom and the Word of Knowledge in that its *object* as well as its operation is entirely supernatural. This is clearly implied in its name, Discerning of SPIRITS. The other revelation Gifts, though equally supernatural in operation, are not equally supernatural in the things they reveal. For the objects of their revelation are often on the natural plane. They may show in a miracle, for instance, a friend confronted with a lion thousands of miles away, or a famine ahead in our own land; both events on the natural plane. But Discerning of Spirits shows in a miracle the Miracle-Source of a miracle, and indicates inerrably its true character, whether heavenly or hellish.

Discerning of Spirits gives supernatural insight into the secret realm of Spirits. It reveals the kind of Spirit that is actuating a person who is manifesting supernatural knowledge or power at the time that the miracle is actually taking place. It supernaturally conveys information that could not be had apart from this Gift. By its operation we may know the true source and nature of any supernatural manifestation, whether divine or satanic, and the character of such spiritual manifestation can only be determined by the use of this Gift. It is not Discernment, but Discerning of Spirits. There is no such gift as the Gift of Discernment. "Discernment" of things other than miracle-working Spirits is the province of the two Gifts we have already considered.

(a) Discerning of Spirits must not be looked upon as a kind of spiritual Thought-Reading.

It is not the revelation of men's thoughts, or hearts, or "spirits" in the metaphorical sense, as when we say a man has "a nasty spirit." That is the same thing as saying he has an ungenerous heart or a selfish disposition. Such characteristics if they are revealed at all would be revealed by a Word of Knowledge. Though the Lord was manifesting a supernatural Gift He was not dealing with a supernatural but a natural manifestation when He said of Nathaniel, "An Israelite indeed, in whom is no guile." And if we speak of Nathaniel, as the Lord did not, as a man of guileless "spirit" we are using the word in a purely figurative sense and applying it to his *character.* A perfectly lawful thing to do so long as we understand what we are doing. But the Gift we are looking at is not Discerning of character or thoughts or hearts, but of Spirits. We must not consider the Gift as a spiritual aid to thought-reading. When Samuel told Saul "all that was in his heart" (1 Samuel ix, 19) he was telling him his thoughts and motives and intentions in a Word of Knowledge, exactly as the Lord was characterizing the thoughts and motives of Nathaniel by the same Gift.

Now there are three kinds of spirit: the divine, the satanic, and the human. (By the human spirit is meant not figuratively a man's disposition, but literally the third part of his tripartite being [I Thess. v, 23.]) Only the first two of these three kinds of Spirit (the divine and the satanic) are supernatural. The human spirit is obviously natural. The Gift of Discerning of Spirits is to distinguish the divine from the satanic while a miracle is being wrought whose source is doubtful to limited human sense. There needs no miraculous Gift to discern the work of the human spirit, for its manifestation is never miraculous. The natural spirit is obviously not supernatural.

The "good spirits" and "evil spirits" of spiritism, supposed to be disembodied human spirits, are a fabrication of the devil. So-called "spirit guides" are foul spirits simulating the spirits of the departed, deceiving human beings: "Familiar spirits." There is only One operative Good Spirit in the Word, the Holy Spirit. Evil spirits are not human spirits nor angelic spirits fallen. They are devilish spirits of satanic origin. The spirits of the just are not floating about in our atmosphere, communicating with the living; they are resting in the presence of Jesus till He come. The spirits of the wicked dead are in Hades fearfully looking for judgment.

A godly commentator says that "the recipients of this Gift could distinguish the real and imaginary possessors of spiritual gifts." But surely that falls short of the mark. The trouble in Corinth and the early Church was not concerning "real and imaginary possessors of spiritual gifts" but between true and false miraculous manifestations equally real, one of divine and the other of satanic origin. An "imaginary" possessor of a gift could work no miracle. But an actual possessor of a counterfeit satanic gift could work mighty miracles. The Gift was, and is, to make the distinction perfectly clear in a miracle of revelation.

Look at the "real" and the "imaginary" in Jeremiah xxviii. Hananiah purports to speak by "the Lord of Hosts, the God of Israel, saying, I have broken the yoke of the king of Babylon . . . within two full years I will bring again into this place all

71

the vessels of the Lord's house ... and I will bring again ... Jeconiah ..." Jeremiah says, by his human spirit, "Amen ... the Lord perform thy words which thou hast prophesied, to bring again the vessels ... and the captives." Then using his own human judgment and cautiously comparing Hananiah's "prophecy" with many such that had gone before and come to nothing, Jeremiah utters as a principle: "When the word of the prophet shall come to pass, then shall the prophet be known, that the Lord hath sent him." "Then the word of the Lord came to Jeremiah," with a *supernatural revelation* and a message to the false prophet, "The Lord hath not sent thee, but thou makest this people to trust in a lie ... this year thou shalt die.... So Hananiah the prophet died the same year."

There is no Discerning of Spirits in all this, but there is a mixture of false and true, natural and supernatural. So far as Hananiah was concerned his false prophecy arose out of his natural mind and his bad heart. It was guesswork, with a false claim to inspiration. It was not a miracle, either false or true. So far as Jeremiah was concerned, his knowledge of Hananiah's perfidy was a Word of Knowledge, while his prophecy of Hananiah's end was a Word of Wisdom. Both miracles.

(b) Discerning of Spirits is not psychological insight.

It is indeed the very reverse of this. Psychological insight, in so far as it is concerned simply with the analysis of human character and mental phenomena, is a development of human powers of judgment. In so far as it is galvanized, so to speak, with a measure of the supernatural, as when a spiritist or a palmist or a crystal-gazer really reveals some secret in a life, that measure of the supernatural has its source in the pit. Remember, however, that many of these magic-mongers are pure frauds, possessing no power of any sort.

Only the three inspirational Gifts, intended for the edification of believers in believers' meetings, operate at the will of man: that is Tongues, Interpretation of Tongues, and Prophecy. The greater Gifts of the Holy Ghost operate only at the Will of the Spirit (1 Cor. xii, 6, 11). Clairvoyance, psychism, hypnotism, magic, occultism, witchcraft, sorcery, spiritism—all these are real supernatural forces producing miracles, but all, responding as they do to the perverted will of man, are satanic in their origin. Discerning of Spirits is designed to strip the mask from such miraculous manifestations and discover behind them Satan and his evil spirits at work.

(c) Discerning of Spirits is not keen mental penetration.

Natural characteristics may be discerned by perfectly innocent natural talent, as of a clever analyst like Dickens. But no natural talent can give power to discern the origin of miraculous manifestations.

(d) Discerning of Spirits is not the power to discover faults in others.

Not one of us requires the baptism in the Holy Spirit to endow us with the gift of criticism and fault-finding. We are all richly endowed by fallen nature with this particular "gift." The use of such a gift is indeed forbidden in the Scriptures. "Judge not, that ye be not judged." One of the purposes of the Holy Ghost baptism is to destroy this gift of criticism and replace it with the sweet "gift" of gentle forbearance. But these things are of course not supernatural at all. This Spiritual Gift is not Discerning of character or of faults, but of SPIRITS.

How often unguarded beginners tell us after their baptism they have received "the gift of discernment!" In substantiation whereof they immediately begin to point out failings in fellow believers! There needs no spiritual gift to uncover human failings, but there needs a good deal of Christly love to cover them.

It is significant that in the same chapter where we are forbidden to find fault with our fellows the Lord Jesus gives us a sure way of estimating sincerity of character. For He will not have His children helplessly deceived. "Beware of false prophets ... Ye shall know them by their fruits" (Matt. vii, 15-20). But this is not Discerning of Spirits. It is not a miracle of revelation. It is an enforced and quite natural self-revelation of the "tree" by the "fruit" which it inevitably produces. The Spirits which are to be discerned by this Gift are those which evidence themselves in supernatural power over human bodies, minds or organs.

The uses of the Gift are obvious; and the present-day uses are the same as the Scriptural.

(1) To help in delivering the afflicted, oppressed, tormented.

Demon possession is responsible today for more cases of mental derangement than most people recognize. For some inscrutable reason there is a general impression that Scripture cases of possession were local and temporary. Why? More infirmities and cruelties and suicides are attributable to evil spirits today than doctors conceive. Minds are still wrecked and driven by "cruel, tormenting spirits" (Mark v, 5; Luke ix, 39), lashing into frenzy, pressing into violent acts and urging to self-destruction. Dreadful asylums are filled with mental wrecks that friends and experts have ceased even to be interested in; men and women who ought to be "loosed" by the Gifts of the Spirit, not "bound with chains" by the helpless authorities. Youthful hearts are driven by "unclean spirits" (Acts v, 16) to revolting talk and obscene behaviour and unspeakable diseases. The power of speech is robbed by "dumb spirits"; the light of day is darkened by "blind spirits"; the voices of beloved friends are muted by "deaf spirits" (Matt. xii, 22; Mark ix, 17, 25); the frames and limbs of beloved mothers and tiny children are distorted and twisted and held by "spirits of infirmity" (Luke xiii, 11, 16). These are all cases not for osteopaths and chiropractors and psychotherapists but for simple believers equipped with the Gifts of the Spirit.

The way of the modern "expert" is sterilization and even a legalized lethal chamber. *Euthanasia.* Vile word.

Take care, modern Uzzahs, how you touch the Ark of God. This is none of your business. It is the priests' affair (2 Samuel vi, 7; Deut. x, 8; Matt. x, 8; Mark xvi, 17). Look in the Book of God. You will find nothing there of your abominable new

"Philistian carts." Take care lest in "steadying" with unholy hands God's holy things you consign to the lethal chamber a flaming evangelist like the Gadarene demoniac (Mark v, 19), or a world-wide preacher of Jehovah's salvation like Nebuchadnezzar (Daniel iv, 31-37). Take care lest you sterilize a deliverer loved of God, a sweet singer, a future parent of the world's wisest philosopher, following a diagnosis as fatuous as the godless King of Gath's (1 Samuel xxi, 13-15). Take care lest you smother in your devil's death box a potential worshipper of the Lord whose alabaster box He had designed should fill the world with fragrance (Mark xvi, 9). The Lord has a purpose concerning devils and imbecility, and you, godless meddler in the purposes of Omniscience! Hands off the holy things, lest you, too, for all your learning and prestige, find a name more execrable and a grave more infamous than Uzzah's!

In response to faith evil spirits will declare their presence and number and names, as the Gadarene demons before the Lord cast them into swinish bodies for destruction. But sometimes it is impossible apart from this Gift to know whether infirmity is the result of diseased organs or arrested functioning; whether sudden, total and incurable deafness, for instance, is the result of crashed aural nerves or simply spirit-power gripping a perfectly normal aural system. Obviously not all impediments are the work of evil spirits, but the Scriptures quoted and several others make it clear that many are. There is a Scripture difference, for instance, between "lunacy" and "demon possession" (Matt. iv, 24). Modern doctors know nothing whatever of these things. Lunacy is sickness of the mind or brain and may be healed by the Gifts of Healings. Demon possession is the occupation by evil spirits of a perfectly healthy body and mind, "swept and garnished" (Matt. xii, 43-45), producing all the effects of derangement. Such possession will never yield to human methods. But *all* sickness whether of mind or body is represented in the Scriptures as "oppression of the devil" (Acts x, 38; Luke xiii, 16), and as such is subject to the corrective energy of the Gifts of the Spirit.

(2) To discover a servant of the devil.

It was when Paul, "filled with the Holy Ghost, set his eyes on" Elymas the sourcerer that he discerned the evil spirits actuating this "child of the devil" (Acts xiii, 9, 10). This was a case of simple discovery, not deliverance. The sin of Elymas was willing and determined subjection to demon authority; hence his terrible punishment of blindness by the hand of the Lord.

(3) To aid in checking the plans of the adversary.

At Philippi a poor young woman "possessed with a spirit of divination" ("python," serpent, Acts xvi, 16) was employed by "that old serpent" to hinder the work of the Lord. After many days enduring the buffets of this "messenger of Satan" Paul discerned the evil spirit and cast it out in the Name of Jesus Christ. Thus a wicked master was deprived of his gains, a wretched woman was delivered from the enemy and the servants of the Lord were ridded of a demon voice that had most subtly endeavoured to subvert the purposes of the Almighty. Unlike wicked Elymas this poor woman was an unwilling agent of the evil one, who had stolen her voice for his evil ends.

(4) To expose plausible error.

"Seducing spirits," "lying spirits," are responsible for "doctrines of devils" and "damnable heresies" (I Tim. iv, 1; 2 Peter ii, 1). There is many a foul demon under a clerical cloak today preaching with pleasing voice and specious illogic lies instead of truth; denying the divinity, the virgin birth, the miracles, the saving blood of the Lord; denying the reality of sin, the devil, divine wrath, coming judgment and eternal hell. And when these devilish doctrines are accompanied as they are in many forms of spiritism with devilish signs and wonders there needs this blessed Gift to discern the evil talon in the soft wool. For the rest the impudent demons are so secure in the appalling general ignorance of the Word of God that they can undisguised and undeterred "deny the Lord that bought" us, as in respectable unitarianism.

(5) To unmask demon miracle-workers.

Wherever there is the true there must of necessity be the false. Satanic "signs and lying wonders" (2 Thess. ii, 9) are the most substantial proof of the existence of the divine, real signs and wonders. The success of the counterfeit is in its likeness to the real. Apart from the Gifts of the Spirit the very saints would be deceived by the "spirits of devils, working miracles" (Rev. xvi, 14). Especially is there need in these tremulous days before blessed Advent that the Church seek the full equipment of the Spirit's supernatural power that we may be enlightened and protected in the face of the increasing frequency and power of Satan's supernatural signs.

We hasten to close this chapter, omitting innumerable modern cases of discernment and deliverance from demon power at home and on the mission fields.

For those not possessing these Gifts God gives a sure way of testing the spirits by making them speak and reveal themselves (1 John iv, 1-6). But notice what is nearly always overlooked, that it is the *"spirits"* themselves, not the persons, that are to be challenged. That means that when the person is actually speaking or acting under supernatural power, as a medium in a seance, the operating spirit must be questioned. It would be useless challenging the same person when not under satanic inspiration, for he would as like as not agree that "Jesus Christ *is* come in the flesh," especially if he suspected that he were under test. But the evil spirit itself would never agree to that foundation truth; hence the blessed certainty of the test.

And Satan does not cast out Satan (Mark iii, 23); that is, evil spirits will not yield to other evil spirits; they will only yield to the servants of God filled with the Holy Ghost (Acts xix, 13-17), and even these must be living in close communion with God (Matt. xvii, 16, 21). Satan, however, may simulate exorcism for his own nefarious ends, as in so-called "christian spiritualism" and "christian science."

Often the testimony of evil spirits is so much like that of the Spirit of God that the true can only be distinguished from the counterfeit by the use of this supernatural Gift. "I know thee, who thou art, the Holy One of God." "These men are the servants of the most high God, which show unto us the way of salvation." True enough testimony, surely! Yet the voices of demons (Mark i, 24; Acts xvi, 17, 18).

Mark the unwisdom of "casting out" spirits without full supernatural assurance of possession, by this Gift. Some are oppressed of the devil, or operated occasionally by spirits from without, "taken with divers torments" (Matt. iv, 24). This oppression or obsession must be distinguished from possession. No suggestion of demon possession should ever be made without the utterest assurance by the voice of the Spirit. And no Christian of course need fear because of the prevalance of these malign agents. Are there not myriads of angelic spirits sent forth to minister for those who are the heirs of salvation, to keep them in all their ways and to deliver them from all evil? Hallelujah!

Then this Gift does not necessarily carry with it the power to exorcise evil spirits even when they are discerned. Gifts of power are requisite in addition, as we shall see later. And notice that Jesus "cast out spirits with His Word." There is no instance of "laying on of hands" for exorcism in the Scripture. We shall do well to follow the pattern in detail.

The very existence of this Gift proves the present reality of evil spirits. They are wrecking and torturing human beings as cruelly as in the Lord's day. At the very foot of the mountain of the Lord's glory they are still throwing men into the water and into the fire and over bridges and under trains and into gas-filled rooms. Dare we come down from the peaks of selfish blessing and spiritual exaltation and seek earnestly such Gifts as will liberate the enslaved from the devil's malign power? The tormented for whom Christ died? Is it fear, or unbelief, or desire for ease in Zion that holds Christendom in the comfortable shelter of its hilltop tabernacles?

CHAPTER SEVEN

One Corinthians Thirteen

LOVE, THE CHARIOTEER

1. Though I speak with the tongues of men and of angels. and have not love, I am become as sounding brass, or a tinkling cymbal.

2. And though I have the gift of prophecy, and understand all mysteries, and all knowledge; and though I have all faith, so that I could remove mountains, and have not love, I am nothing.

3. And though I bestow all my goods to feed the poor, and though I give my body to be burned, and have not love, it profiteth me nothing.

One Corinthians Thirteen is not an interlude: it is an interlink, It is not the impatient laying aside of a task by one who has grown rather weary of it and rather afraid of its intricacy and consequences. It is not a collapse, a defeat, a capitulation, so to speak, in the arena of the supernatural. It is rather the second vital lap of three in the same event over the same course. It is not a digression from the supernatural theme, a change of direction in the voyage over miraculous seas. Chapter thirteen is an intensification of the same theme as chapters twelve and fourteen; a speeding-up of the identical ship in the original direction. Paul had not, as it were, tired of his voyage in perilous seas and suddenly headed his craft for sunnier climes and safer shores. That is how the frightened commentators look at it. Let us bring our metaphor up to date and say that rather had he fixed his helm to a rigid course and conducted his passenger-pupils below decks, to show them in the crammed fire-holes of the engine room the secret of his brave ship's performance. While there, however, he stays for a moment to hearten the stokers for the roughest stretch of the voyage that lies ahead of them in chapter fourteen, thus providing his pupils with gratuitous lessons in engineering as well as navigation. For while one is necessary to make the ship go, the other is necessary to make it go right. Gifts AND Love, Love AND Gifts. That is how the Lord wishes His ship to come into port,

One Corinthians Thirteen is not a Dissertation on Love. The subject of the chapter is not Love. The subject is: Love, the True Motive of Spiritual Gifts. The comparison is not between Spiritual Gifts and Love, as is almost universally taught; but between Spiritual Gifts WITHOUT Love and Spiritual Gifts WITH Love!

In an earlier chapter I have suggested that it is thoroughly unscriptural to treat the Nine Gifts as nine-pins and scatter them with Love. That is to make God the author of confusion. Rather should they be regarded as royal steeds of the King's chariot in the careful control of Love the Charioteer. The last verse of chapter twelve exhorts us to take up the Gifts and give them to Love for control. The first verse of chapter fourteen, reversing the order but keeping the thought, says Get Love and give it the Gifts for its task. The whole of chapter thirteen deals with Gifts in the hands of Love or Love in charge of the Gifts. So are the three chapters inseparably linked. Without Love the Gifts are wilful and wayward. Without the Gifts Love is unoccupied (so far as the Miracle side of its manifold duties is concerned). With both Gifts and Love the Lord is able by the Spirit to give miracle-Light at its brightest and miracle-Power at its fullest for those in darkness and distress. Surely that is the message of the chapter.

One is almost driven to believe that the misrepresentations of this chapter are deliberate. Verse one does not say that speaking with other tongues is vain because spectacular and love admirable because unobtrusive I have known most unobtrusive speaking with tongues and revoltingly spectacular "love". What the verse does imply is that speaking with tongues without love will not profit the SPEAKER WITH TONGUES. "*I* [not Tongues] am becoming as sounding brass."

But I have never seen more real love anywhere than among those people who speak with other tongues, and I do not recall being impressed with the prevalence of love among those Christians who violently oppose the Gifts of the Spirit. "You follow after Gifts—I'll follow after Love," they say in effect, forgetting that the absence of Gifts does not mean the presence of Love. Following after Love means desiring Spiritual Gifts. "You keep your Gifts," I heard a woman once saying: "we have our holiness." As though the two were opposed! A distressful example of unholiness. For Spiritual Gifts are an essential part of true Scriptural holiness. To prove that is the whole purpose of the three chapters we are considering. So that we might reverently add, in the true spirit of these three verses, that Though I *claim* the love of the Beloved Disciple and have not Love, it profiteth me nothing.

Then personally I do not think the verse implies that men can under inspiration speak with angel tongues. Paul is just using a strong figure to intensify the force of his statement. "Though I *do* speak with human tongues I have never learned—indeed, I *might be able* to speak with angel's languages ..." is what Paul means. As when on another occasion for the sake of argument he takes a hypothetical case of angels preaching false gospels — not that he really means that angels do such dreadful things. He just wishes to enforce a strong point in his argument (Gal. i, 8).

Then verse two does not say that Love is superior to the Gifts of Prophecy, Word of Wisdom ("mysteries"), Word of Knowledge, Miracle-working Faith; neither does it say that these Gifts are profitless without Love; what it does say is that without Love the POSSESSOR of these Gifts is not profited in their employment. "I [not the Gifts] am nothing."

In substantiation of which verse three, leaving Spiritual Gifts, applies the same principle to other and non-supernatural things. For it is not only authentic Spiritual Gifts that are rendered profitless by the absence of Love, but also authentic philanthropy and authentic martyrdom. Love is not put in the scale against philanthropy and martyrdom and thus declared to be comparatively beyond them, as though they were superseded by Love, Love, indeed, is seen to be the actuating

81

principle that renders philanthropy profitable to the philanthropist and martyrdom profitable to the martyr and both acceptable to God. The same with Spiritual Gifts. Love is not put in the scale against them and seen to be superior in comparison. Love is seen to be the actuating principle that renders Spiritual Gifts not authentic, nor important—for their authenticity and importance are not in question—but profitable. Profitable, that is, to the Operator of the Gifts. For our use of Spiritual Gifts might enormously profit others, in heavenly illumination and deliverance; yet, if the motive is not love, the very gifts we employ for others' blessing will be without profit to ourselves.

Philanthropy in any case—love or no love—profits the beneficiary. A legacy of £10,000 of course will profit the legatee, whether it was bequeathed in love or vainglory. Paul never says that philanthropy profits nothing, even without love. He says, "Without love it profits ME nothing." But philanthropy which streams from Love as its source profits beneficiary and benefactor alike. So with Spiritual Gifts. Care must be taken to employ them in such a manner as that while profiting others they shall not be unprofitable to us. How tragic for one in possession of the Gifts of Healings, for instance, to be instrumental in delivering a sufferer instantaneously from deadly disease, and yet to be himself without profit in spite of his authentic divine Gifts! Gifts, like Goodness, are the expression of divine Love. Love must be the operating principle not only of Goodness but of Gifts.

LOVE, THE LOVELIEST

4 Love suffereth long, and is kind; love envieth not; love vaunteth not itself, is not puffed up.

5 Doth not behave itself unseemly, seeketh not her own, is not easily provoked, thinketh no evil;

6 Rejoiceth not in iniquity, but rejoiceth in the truth;

7 Beareth all things, believeth all things, hopeth all things, endureth all things.

Love is the loveliest thing in heaven or out of it. It heads the list of lovely things in Galatians v, 22, 23. But though it heads the list it does not include or exclude all other lovely things. Look at the delightful bouquet of them with Love as the Rose of Beauty, Love, joy, peace, long-suffering, gentleness, goodness, faith, meekness, temperance. But there is a difference between this ninefold Fruit and the ninefold Gifts we have been considering. Every member of this ninefold Fruit is to be represented in every individual Christian, whereas the Nine Gifts are distributed among the members of the Church, one here and one there. Fruit is to be deliberately produced by the aid of the Spirit but at the will of each believer. Gifts can only be received by each at the Will of the Spirit. An individual's Spiritual Gift may enjoy perfect expression though it is a solitary one in him. But no fruit can enjoy perfect expression in any individual if it is not accompanied by every other member of the list. Love, for instance, is not complete if it has not "long-suffering" for fellow. That is the statement both of Galatians and Corinthians. "Love suffereth long." Love, again, is not complete if it is not accompanied by "faith." That, too, is the declaration of both Epistles. Love "believeth all things." Love, once more, is not perfect love without "meekness." Love "vaunteth not itself, is not puffed up," says Corinthians. And so on. In that sense this portion is a repetition of the Galatian list, save that here all Fruit of the Spirit is seen to be summed up in Love the chiefest.

Now a character may be complete with but one Gift and that at least — speaking with tongues; but a character can never be complete with but one Fruit, though that one be the greatest, even Love. Let present-day "Corinthians" who boast in the possession of Spiritual Gifts and use them selfishly — get Love, with all its lovely associates. And let present-day "Corinthians" who boast in their possession of Love without its sister Fruit, and moreover without Gifts — get the remaining Fruit and get Gifts, according to the Scriptures they preach. For if they neither speak with tongues nor are "kind" they are farther from the Scripture pattern than the fellow Christian who both speaks with tongues "and is kind." And his kindness is, moreover, a better recommendation of Love than their absence of tongues.

To repeat: this chapter is not a Rhapsody on Love. Or if it is a rhapsody on Love it is a rhapsody on Related Love. Love Related to Spiritual Gifts. The Love that Paul is writing about is the love which will cause possessors of Spiritual Gifts to employ them edifyingly, and stir up non-possessors of the Gifts to covet them earnestly. All the time in the chapter he has his eye on Spiritual Gifts. He is thinking of the Purity of the Body, and the Unity of the Body, just as he was in chapter twelve. And he is also thinking of the Power of the Body, as he was in chapter twelve. He has his eye on helplessness as well as schism, knowing that the absence of power by no means implies the presence of unity—more likely even the negation of it.

Every clause of this portion, verses four to seven, has designed reference not only to Love but to Spiritual Gifts, the subject of all these three Corinthian chapters. Just as chapters twelve and fourteen contain a corrective for Gifts in practice—Gifts competitive, schismatic, disorderly, or even absent—so this portion contains a corrective for Love the motive—Love selfish, critical, disorderly, or even absent. For it does not seem to strike some critics that Love in Corinth was just as disorderly as Gifts and that one disorder was the cause of the other. Whereas that is the whole meaning of these present verses. And is it not true that sometimes what passes for love today is just as disorderly: sentiment, selfishness, extravagent natural affection, sectarian clannishness, or even that narrow exclusiveness that is inspired by a common dislike—I had almost said a common hate? And of course such disorderly love can be found both inside and outside Pentecost—both in those who according to the Scriptures speak with other tongues and those who contrary to Scripture forbid to speak with tongues. But:

"Love suffereth long." Beareth long, that is, not only with those who do not hold its views of the Gifts, but with those who do and make fuller use of the Gifts, as, well as those who through timidity hesitate to employ the Gifts they possess.

"And is kind" -to those who, like Paul and thousands today, speak with tongues; to those who, on the contrary, do not speak with tongues though they might (xiv, 5). Kind even to those who obviously have supernatural power, and even to those who obviously have not.

"Love envieth not" those who possess the larger Gifts nor yet those who because they have only the lesser Gifts have greater public prominence or greater liberty of expression. Envieth not those who seem to have a wider following because they despise the whole of the Gifts. Envieth not the door-keeper because he prophesies nor the elder because he has the Gifts of Healings.

"Love vaunteth not itself": does not boast itself up though it possesses six Gifts, or though it possesses none! Love brags not in making a counter claim of Love against Gifts. For remember there is far more likelihood of presumption in claiming Love than Gifts, for Gifts are a presentation without merit, while Love is an acquisition with merit.

"Is not puffed up"; literally "breathed or blown up or inflated" like a clown's bladder. For what is there to be puffed up about though we possess the Nine Gifts? Are they not all GIFTS and operations of the SPIRIT bestowed on us without reference to merit? Or whatever is there to boast about if we possess none of the Gifts we are expressly told to covet? And in any case is not to be puffed up to appear absurd? And is not all this an echo of chapter twelve?

"Doth not behave itself unseemly," in the Assembly by giving way to authentic inspiration in a disorderly manner, or even in deliberately suppressing authentic Gifts at the proper time for manifestation. This surely is a deliberate anticipation of chapter fourteen.

"Seeketh not her own." Seeketh not her own glory in the showy exercise of the more public Gifts. Seeketh not her own ease in escaping obligation either to seek Gifts or to employ Gifts possessed.

"Is not easily provoked": not "greatly excited" under unction, nor distressed by powerful manifestations of real inspiration in others. Love is not upset by spiritual manifestations that are beyond its present knowledge or experience. Love learns in calm but zealous repose.

"Thinketh no evil" of those who use Gifts regularly or even of those who write unscriptural volumes against them.

"Rejoiceth not in iniquity," which, sad to tell, may still as in Corinth consort even with authentic Gifts as well as with the absence of them.

"But rejoiceth in [or with] the truth," either when it is manifest in purged individual or assembly life, or when it is evident in utterance or revelations in the Spirit. As well as when it is proclaimed in the spoken Word in the pulpit.

"Beareth all things." Two closely related meanings are possible here. Beareth all things, even certain excesses sometimes evident in those who, like children with new toys, have not long been in possession of their Baptism in the Spirit and some altogether delightful Spiritual Gift. Or "closely covereth" certain unedifying displays of Spiritual Gifts, lovingly ready to admit the reality of the Gift and to credit the user with a desire to improve with experience. Disorder is bad. Death is worse. Do not let us demand the order of the parade ground in the face of the enemy's flying bullets. The newspapers recorded only last week (2/2/34) how that in the great war four hundred precious young lives were massacred under enemy fire while some maniac of Order was yelling at his men to "form fours—pile arms—dress by the right—place equipment at feet"—etc.! And this unhappy company were ironically part of a battalion called "The King's Own"! Let us neither massacre the precious Gifts with disorder nor expose them to massacre by unreasonable demands for order.

"Believeth all things"; even the urgency of the divine command to desire Spiritual Gifts. Even the sincerity of fellow Christians who promote Gifts, and often the sincerity of those who in error oppose them.

"Hopeth all things." Love hopeth that all the Nine Gifts shall be in manifestation in every assembly of God's people in every church and denomination as in Corinth. Hopeth that all the present opposers of Pentcost shall be filled with the same blessed Spirit and equipped with the same mighty and glorious Gifts. Hopeth that the Lord will bring deadness to life, disorder to order, helplessness to power, formality to reality in all places where men call upon Him in truth. Hopeth that many bitter critics are really sweet at heart. Hopeth that in any case the Pentecostal people will sweep forward to the possession of every good Gift for the furtherance of God's blessed plans for complete redemption.

"Endureth all things." That is "remaineth under" certain things as under a burden rather than drive out the miraculous power of God or put out the fire in young zealots or dry up the fountain in arid wastes of spiritual stodginess. It is easier to extinguish a fire than to kindle it. A sure way to obviate the necessity of fire stations is to abolish firegrates. Love endureth all things rather than slay God's living Gifts with a critical stare or a cruel misrepresentation or a violent ostracism. Love endureth all things moreover rather than "seek her own" triumph in controversy either way. And Love endureth hearty praises in the lusty saint as well as silent adoration in the contemplative one.

This love, though it does not appear among the Gifts, must appear in the midst of the Gifts. Yes; Love is the fairest blossom in the garden. It lends its fragrance even to the kitchen garden, though it does not grow there. Can we say that the flower garden is for orderly beauty while the kitchen garden is for orderly power. If so can we not add that Gifts overblown by the fragrance of Love are for beautiful orderly power? For love works no miracles without Gifts. Miracles, however, become superlative in the hands of excelling Love.

Such is this divine Love, the greatest of all forces for the handling of the Gifts. And when we have considered it as the grand motive of Spiritual Gifts, as Paul does in this chapter, we can proceed to apply it just as definitely to the wider and more general affairs of our Christian walk and warfare.

To sum up: Love is the loveliest, in obedience to the Altogether Lovely. Love immediately accepts the Word of the

THE GIFTS OF THE SPIRIT

Fairest and runs to do His behest. Love therefore desires Spiritual Gifts. Love earnestly covets the best Gifts. Love despises not prophesyings. Love covets to prophesy. Love forbids not to speak with tongues. Love would never dream of neglecting Spiritual Gifts. Wherefore, beloved disciple of the Lord, follow after Love and desire Spiritual Gifts.

GIFTS AT THE GATE

8 Love never faileth: but whether there be prophecies, they shall fail; whether there be tongues, they shall cease; whether there be knowledge, it shall vanish away.

In the first part of this chapter we saw the necessity of *One* to handle the Gifts in a masterly and orderly way. In the second part this desirable One steps down from heaven, as it were, and displays His lovely characteristics and qualifications for the high task. Finally, in this third part, we look to the end of His lovely ministrations and behold Him halt His Team at the portal of the eternal city of light. So that, to make another and final use of our metaphor (with your patience), we can say that Love drives the steed to the Gate. There the chariot takes wings and enters without them. The Charioteer is seen to take lovely Shape and shining Vesture. His name passes from seraph to seraph. It swells upon a thousand tongues. JESUS! The Gifts are lost in the Giver. Knowledge in Light. Miracles in Wonder. Becoming in Being. Part in Perfection. Loving in LOVE.

But that is ahead of us—as we write. Till "that which is perfect is come," when He who is perfect is Come Again! Perhaps till the Millennium has rolled away its joyous and care-free years. We are not yet at the Gate. The Gifts in the hands of Love are the Lord's plan till He come.

Verse eight, we see, displays a contrast. Between the imperishable nature of Love and the impermanence of Spiritual Gifts. Prophecy, tongues, knowledge. These shall fail, cease, vanish away. Our friends the critics of Pentecost repeatedly emphasize the ephemeral character of the first two. Let me emphasize also the impermanence of the third: knowledge. There is a sort of implication abroad that we are cherishing in prophecy and tongues things that are worthless because impermanent, while our critics are pursuing in "knowledge" something that is invaluable because enduring. "Whether there be knowledge it shall vanish away" is the clear statement of the Word.

First let us say that Gifts by their very nature are impermanent because they are fragments of a coming Whole; but they are none the less essential for the period over which they are designed to be operative. The very virtue of a Spiritual Gift is in its impermanence, as the virtue of an acorn is in its impermanence. To make permanent the acorn would be to extinguish oak forests for ever. To make permanent the Gifts would be to ensure merely fragmentary knowledge and power for ever. To sacrifice an acorn is to get a forest hanging thick with them. To look to the "end" of Spiritual Gifts is to took to the great Whole of which they are but the fragmentary representatives and samples.

Impermanence is not a fault. It is merely a necessary characteristic of some very delightful things. The Gifts of the Spirit are ephemeral like the faculties of the body. But no man neglects his eyesight because of its impermanence. Rather the reverse. Eyesight, like Spiritual Gifts, belongs to the temporal part-knowledge stage of our eternal development. But who gouges out his eyes or cuts off his ears because he accepts the superior importance of spirit or mind or soul? When that which is perfect is come we shall not need Spiritual Gifts—nor ears of flesh. We need both at present. Gifts or no Gifts here, we shall all be endowed with marvellous wisdom and power hereafter. But shall we neglect the opportunity God gives us in the Gifts to help with miracles in the edification of ourselves and the building up of His Church and the deliverance of the needy NOW? Was the Lord Jesus really mocking us when He promised that miracles should be wrought in His Name (Mark xvi, 16)? The Gift is the only chance of a miracle NOW. Heaven is a continuous and superlative series of miracles.

But Love never endeth. Love commences its full-grown

eternal course here and now. We need not have fragmentary Love, praise God, but Love abounding and full according to our capacity. God gives Gifts (revelation and energy) by measure now, but Love without measure to overflow every heart. Love, like grace, is superabounding. This partial temporal power and insight in the hands of this abounding and enduring Love is the Christian's perfect equipment till Jesus comes.

9 For we know in part, and we prophecy in part.
10 But when that which is perfect is come, then that which is in part shall be done away.
11 When I was a child, I spake as a child, I understood as a child, I thought as a child; but when I became a man, I put away childish things.
12 For now we see through a glass, darkly; but then face to face: now I know in part; but then shall I know even as also I am known.

As verse eight shows the contrast between temporal Gifts and enduring Love this portion shows the reason for that difference and gives a delightful illustration to help us.

Gifts do not terminate in the simple sense usually conveyed by the commentators. Gifts only cease in the sense that they are swallowed up in the Whole of which they are a part. It is not a bad thing but a good thing to possess NOW a part of that divine ability which we shall have for ever. It is a thing to covet earnestly. So that our figure of the Charioteer and His Team is not the best we could have. It serves to illustrate Control. But here we have Metamorphosis as well. The best figure of course is the one God gives us in this marvellous portion. It is the simple figure of a child growing up into a man. Gifts are only done away as a child is done away when he becomes a man. The child remains though he vanishes in the man. No man slays his child or neglects him or vilifies him in entranced anticipation of the day when he will be a man! "When I was a child, I spake as a child, I understood as a child, I thought as a child." That is—spake, understood, reasoned miraculously through the Gifts as a SUPERNATURAL "child." With God's speech, understanding, reason. Do *you* speak with miracle tongues and see even "darkly" with miracle eyes—you, CHILD of God in your present temporal child stage? How can you "put away" these "childish things" when you have never possessed them—never even "desired" them —perhaps even derided them and those who have them? For let me courteously repeat for the sake of clearness that these Corinthian chapters are written to those who are in actual POSSESSION of Miracle-Gifts, that they may know how profitably to employ them. Those who have never received the Baptism in the Spirit; those who therefore do not possess Spiritual Gifts—these do not "speak" nor "understand" nor "reason" nor "see through a glass" nor "know in part" "as a child" at all in the sense of this chapter.

And notice that when Paul says he "put away childish things" (referring to that future day when we shall "put away" Gifts) he is not using the word "childish" in the sense of puerile or silly, but merely in the sense of elementary or incomplete. The Greek word used here for "child" means a babe "without full measure of speech," says Young. Implying a nucleus that will one day develop. But do not let us despise our babe's measure of speaking with tongues because in the perfect Day we shall employ heaven's perfect vocabulary for ever. It is a gross—and I almost said deliberate—misrepresentation of the text to suggest that this portion teaches that speaking with tongues is infantile and therefore undesirable, while "preaching" and "knowledge" are mature and therefore desirable. "Prophecy" has nothing whatever to do with "preaching," and "knowledge" has nothing to do with mental attainments either secular or theological. The application of Paul's metaphor is fairly stated as follows: "Now I am in my child-stage of spiritual equipment I speak with tongues by the Spirit, I have a Word of Knowledge or a Word of Wisdom by the Spirit; but when I arrive at maturity in heaven's eternal state my baby lispings will be lost in Speech and my baby revelations will be swallowed up in Revelation. All my brightest spiritual 'peerings,' which after all are but as imperfect reflections in an improvised mirror, will one day be transformed into 'seeings' in the Light as God sees, and all my stammerings will be developed into articulate speaking out of the full Knowledge that God my Father ever possesses." Has the reader commenced even to peer or stammer in the Spirit, as he might by the fullness of the Spirit and His supernatural manifestations?

And what is the mystery in the seeming contradiction, "Whether there be knowledge, it shall vanish away" and "Then shall I know even as also I am known"? The answer to this query will provide a key to the mystery of the "passing" of all the other Gifts.

Here is a Knowledge that both passes away and abides for ever. What knowledge is it that displays such strange characteristics? There are three kinds of knowledge: (1) Natural, human, erring knowledge. (2) Divine knowledge. (3) Miraculous knowledge.

No. (1) is not this knowledge. Much that is called human knowledge will never get into heaven at all. Scientific and psychological and philosophical and theological vapourings and imaginings. In God's sight such is not knowledge, but ignorance—and even worse than that—folly, the reverse of knowledge. Such knowledge does not "vanish away" in the Scripture sense. It never commences in any eternal sense. It is not knowledge (1 Cor. i, 20; iii, 19). It is not this human so-called "knowledge" that will be lost in the great augmentation in the Glory. This is not the part-knowledge spoken of in the chapter.

Then No. (2), Divine knowledge, incomplete but real knowledge of God's will and ways and Word is not the knowledge that "vanishes away." For surely this we carry with us into heaven. To know God in this way IS life eternal (John xvii, 3).

What is that "knowledge" that shall "vanish away" and yet leave us with a "knowing" so clear that it is in our measure even as God's? "We shall know even as also we are known."

Surely this knowledge is No. (3), Miracle-Knowledge, now fragmentary, then full and complete. Now we know (supernaturally) in part—if we possess the appropriate Gifts of the

Spirit. This knowledge is miraculous knowledge—not the preacher's nor the teacher's nor the scientist's, but the SEER'S, who knows in part the thoughts of the heart like Samuel, or in measure the future like Agabus. That Knowledge which is now hidden from the natural senses or faculties at their highest; that fragment of God's Miracle-Knowledge which we have distributed to us by His Spirit in the Miracle Gifts. Logically this is the part-knowledge that must eventually be lost or caught up in the Whole. It is only this part-knowledge that "vanishes away." The Whole, of which it is a temporary fragment, endures. In that sense KNOWLEDGE, like Love, "never faileth."

To sum up: human "knowledge" being foolishness never commences. Divine knowledge never ceases. The only knowledge that both ceases and endures is Supernatural Knowledge conveyed by the Gifts of the Spirit.

13 And now abideth faith, hope, love, these three; but the greatest of these is love.

"These three" are the immortal *enduring* things that stand in contrast to the blessed but *temporal* Gifts. "These THREE" are enduring, eternally abiding, not just One of them, though that be the great First. We are not to read into this verse, as many do, that Faith will be lost in sight and Hope in actuality while Love will alone endure. All the members of this heavenly trinity are equally imperishable. Faith will be for ever the basis of our enjoyment of God. Enduring Faith. Hope will be for ever the forward projection of that Faith into the infinite future. Unquenchable Hope. While LOVE the Greatest, will be unchangeably that in which all things subsist, even Faith and Hope; for Love is not only OF God, as Faith is, and Hope; but verily GOD IS LOVE. Love without end. Hallelujah! Amen.

CHAPTER EIGHT

The Gifts of Healings

. . . to another the gifts of healings. 1 Cor. xii, 9.

WE now come to the second group of Spiritual Gifts. The three Gifts of Power. Among these, Healings is the most widely distributed. From which we gather it is the least of the Gifts in its own group. It will be profitable to consider this before the two greater Gifts of Power: Miracles and Faith.

First we must notice the important plurality in its title. It is not the Gift of Healing. It is the Gifts of Healings. Three times in this twelfth chapter it is mentioned (9, 28, 30) and each time in the original the two nouns are in the plural. This plurality is seen only in verse 28 in our rendering. It is the only Gift of the nine which is in itself a series. Each of the others is a Gift. This is "Gifts." But for the sake of keeping it clear from the other eight we will still refer to "it" when convenient as "a Gift" as though like the remainder it were in the singular.

These Gifts are for the supernatural healing of diseases and infirmities without natural means of any sort. They are the miraculous manifestation of the Spirit for the banishment of all human ills whether organic, functional or nervous; acute or chronic. Whatever difficulty writers have discovered in defining other Gifts of the Spirit, this particular Gift is understood by all. The Lord Jesus Himself forced it into prominence by the innumerable deliverances He wrought by it in His public ministry and in the authority He gave His disciples to accomplish the same beneficent works through the same endowment. The command to "heal the sick" stands in the van of the royal commission He gave them, that their divine words might be confirmed as they preached by miraculous signs and wonders (Matt. x, 8). This is the Gift that more than any lifted common fishermen and artisans into prominence in the early Christian Church while the envious professionals were wilting under the exposure of their failure, in the light of these non-professional triumphs.

And once again, as in all the other Gifts, we must emphasize the entirely supernatural character of the Gift. For these Gifts of Healings are commonly confused with a high degree of medical or surgical or manipulative or scientific ability These are all of the natural man. They do not occur in the Scriptures at all, except as they are superseded in Christ. Healings through these Gifts are wrought by the power of Christ through the Spirit, by ignorant believers with no knowledge of physiology, diseases, symptoms, drugs or surgery. True, Luke the beloved physician was among the Lord's disciples. So was John the beloved fisherman. As the one became a spiritual fisher and supernatural healer, so the other became a supernatural healer and spiritual fisher. It is entirely dishonest to suggest as some writers do that Paul took Luke with him on his journeys as a safeguard, in case his miraculous Gifts failed! Those who know God's miraculous ways in the Scriptures look upon such a statement as an impossible travesty of the truth. For all God's Miracle-Gifts work only according to *faith*. Means, such as Luke's supposititious medicine chest, are the very opposite of faith. Unbelief, in short. The Gifts of the Spirit do not work *with* means but without them. The sin in Abraham that delayed the birth of Isaac until it was put away was the "means" he provided as a resort in case the miracle of the promise failed to work. While Hagar was behind the door, so to speak, as an aid to God in the fulfilment of His promise that promise could not possibly be fulfilled. The miracle eventually transpired, not through expedients or partial means, but through *faith* alone. When Luke the physician followed Jesus he no longer used medicines and media; he healed like the other disciples (if he healed at all) by the laying on of hands and anointing with oil. When Paul and Luke, and others, arrived at the island of Melita and found people desperately sick, it was not Luke the physician with his medicine chest who healed them, but Paul the tentmaker by the laying on of hands and the working of these mighty Gifts.

While we hope we should be among the last to speak disparagingly of hospitals, or of doctors and nurses who give so unsparingly of their time and efforts for the alleviation of human suffering, yet we must most emphatically state that modern medicine is not the legitimate fulfilment of Jesus' command to "heal the sick." Rather is it the negation, the neglect, if not the positive denial of it. And this is equally true of genuinely born-again "Christian doctors." The only "Christian physicians" acknowledged in the Scriptures are those ordinary believers who heal miraculously through these Gifts, or equally miraculously through the laying on of hands or anointing with oil. The supposition that the Lord Jesus heals today through Harley Street is no more Scriptural than the claim that He saves through Oxford. Medicine and surgery is the world's way. God's way, the only way revealed in the Word, is healing by supernatural divine power. These two ways are entirely opposed. True, many real Christians resort to the way of the unbeliever, but that does not alter the fact that it is the way of the unbeliever. Divine healing is the only healing authorized by the Scriptures. Medical healing is not, as some people declare, "God's second best." It is entirely of the educated world. God has no second best.

True it is that even in human healing God is the source. Last year I had the pleasure of hearing one of the world's "greatest preachers." He was expounding most profitably the one hundred and third Psalm. When he came to the much cherished third verse, "Who healeth all thy diseases," his hearty comment was, "I believe in divine healing." At this a brother in the front (whom I judged, of course, to be Pentecostal. No. It was not I!) shouted a lusty Hallelujah! This ejaculation in the dead silence of that respectable nonconformist congregation produced a mild consternation, and directed all eyes, including the somewhat apprehensive speaker's, upon the inspired and perfectly Scriptural "delinquent." "But then," continued the preacher with an air of assured defiance, "I believe *all* healing is divine!" There was of course an amused titter going round the crowded pews of even that orderly church. A titter which grew boldly into an undisguised chorus of laughter when the speaker demanded, addressing the solitary son of Jehoshaphat, "Why don't you shout Hallelujah now?"

My hearty sympathy was on the side of the good Pentecostal praiser, not only in his original outburst of praise, but in his subsequent silence as this dart from the opponent's bow whizzed noisily and flashily wide of its destined mark. For to cry Hallelujah at that statement would be to seem to approve the statement as the speaker *said* it, whereas it is only true in a sense that would have needed more time for explanation that courtesy permitted in the circumstances. The statement was certainly not true in the meaning of the Psalmist's verse, nor, logically, of the speaker's original comment.

In an ultimate sense, of course, all healing is of God. But then in this ultimate sense all sickness is likewise of God, and all everything else, except sin. "I kill, and I make alive; I wound, and I heal" is Jehovah's declaration (Deut. xxxii, 39). "In faithfulness hast thou afflicted me" admits the Psalmist. But that is not quite what the speaker meant, is it? Should that brother, the great preacher, by any miracle of Providence read these simple lines, let him consider himself affectionately rebuked for his too obvious departure from even the rudiments of logic in such a showy delivery of an arrow! God bless him and all his beloved but illogical confreres, and bring them into this glorious Pentecostal experience!

If medical practice were really the continuation of Christ's beneficent work, as in many quarters it is claimed to be, the work would be done freely, as the preaching of the gospel ought still to be, as both actually were in the Lord Jesus' day and in the day of the early Christians. True the labourer (workman) is still worthy of his hire (meat). But that "hire" in the Scripture never means more than bread for the hour. Then how can doctors claim that they are doing the Lord's work when they neither serve Him nor believe in Him in many cases, and when they unblushingly call in the aid of the Christ-rejecting world in support of their work and efforts? Can the holy Lord really receive the gains of ungodly "sweepstakes" and stage-celebrity auctions and music hall iniquities? And how can a man who knows how such money is raised call himself a Christian doctor while he has part in such ungodly methods, and fellowship with such unscrupulous men on equal terms without protest? Has the Lord really given over His beloved sick to the world, and His precious Gifts of Healings to the ungodly who reject His grace daily and even blaspheme His holy Name?

Believers will recall two attractive pictures, illustrating Christ the Saviour and Christ the Healer respectively. Do they ever notice the inconsistency in comparison? The Saviour picture shows a number of lovely children clambering happily around the seated Christ. Beautiful. The other, however, shows a number of sick children with one obviously ready to die in the foreground. But this time instead of the Christ there is a young doctor in white overalls with his ugly instruments and phials exposed at his feet, and the Lord Jesus *a shadowy figure in the background!* Is not this an exact representation of the position of Christ in the healing of men today? But to make these two pictures agree ought not the Christ, not the doctor, to be the prominent figure as the Healer, with the sick children being healed as of old by His divine touch alone, even as the lost are saved by His divine hand alone? Or the other way about, ought not the happy children in the Saviour picture to be clambering round a nun or a priest with Christ a shadowy figure in the background—as He actually is today, in many quarters, with regard both to salvation and healing?

No thinking person can really believe that poisonous drugs and cruel scalpels have anything to do with *divine* healing. To put it quite reasonably, with no shadow of intended offence, surely medicine at its best is merely a development of the world's ever-changing and ever-futile attempts to wipe out disease. As this generation laughs at the methods of the last, surely a wise man can see that the next generation will laugh (if the Lord tarry) at the methods of today. Is it not obvious that the Lord God has His hand on the world? And is it not possible that He Himself wonders at human attempts to rid the world of disease—in order that ungodly men might be at ease in ignoring Him and mocking at His blessed Son and His merciful salvation? And is the world really more healthy today after all men's efforts than it was when our grandparents lived? Is it not just that as one disease begins to relax its mortifying hold another more terrible most relentlessly adjusts its grasp?

The Lord still has compassion on the sick. He still has a way of deliverance from the power of the enemy. It is still the way revealed in His Word. The sick will do well to seek it out and bring their diseases to Him as the distressed their maladies of old. It is a safe way; a painless way; a free way and a holy way. Because it is HIS way.

It will help us to understand the workings and purpose of these Gifts of Healings if we consider some of their uses in the Scriptures.

(a) First of all they are to deliver the sick and destroy the works of the devil in the human body.

The Scriptures are full of examples. What a blessed relief for the incurably sick to know that like the leper of old they can come to One who will not cast them off. And if there are those who have been put off by the enemy's suggestion that though the Lord CAN heal them it may not be HIS WILL to heal them—let them read for themselves, now, the repeated "I WILL" in Matthew viii, 3 and 7, and take heart as they believe that that test question and answer were put in the Word for our encouragement today. It is THE LORD'S DECLARED WILL to heal the sick. But they must come to HIM in the way plainly indicated in the WORD.

As of old "Jesus of Nazareth . . . went about doing good and healing all who were oppressed of the devil" (Acts x, 38), so today He is going about with Spirit-filled believers continuing His ministry of healing as He promised, through these Gifts.

(b) To establish Jesus' astonishing claims.

How can men really be convinced that Jesus has power to forgive sinners' sins? Here at His feet is a dreadful case—paralysed in body and sick in soul. Which would be the "easier" task: to heal his paralysis or forgive his sins? Surely power to work the one miracle involves power to work the other! That all may know for ever that Jesus has power to forgive sins He says to the palsied one, Arise, and he immediately arises.

"Priest" in your "confessional," when you can in public say to the hopelessly paralytic, Arise!—*and he arises whole*—we may be willing to consider 'your claim to remit men's sins according to the Lord's declaration. Not before. One is as "easy" as the other. But *talk* is neither healing nor remission.

"Say ye ... Thou blasphemest; because I said, I am the Son of God? If I do not the works of my Father, believe me not. But if I do, though ye believe not me, believe the works" (John x, 36-38). Transcendent mystery of the divine Sonship of Jesus confirmed by transcendent works of healing! Ought not such claims to be attested by similar signs today?

(c) To authorize the gospel message as preached by God's servants.

"And now Lord, behold their threatenings," prayed Peter when preaching the pure gospel (as it always will do) had brought the religious formalists' anger upon his head, "and grant unto thy servants that with all boldness they may speak thy word, by stretching forth thy hand to heal; and that signs and wonders may be done by the name of thy holy child Jesus" (Acts iv, 29,30). How swift was the divine response! "With great power gave the apostles witness ... And by the hand of the apostles were many signs and wonders wrought among the people" (Acts iv, 33; v, 12).

And later in Philip's ministry "the people with one accord gave heed unto those things which Philip spake, hearing and seeing the miracles which he did. For unclean spirits ... came out ... and many taken with palsies, and that were lame, were healed" (Acts viii, 6, 7). Is there less need for miracles to confirm the gospel message in the ungodly unbelieving world today? Less need than in Capernaum or Corinth or Samaria or Sarepta?

(d) To establish the Resurrection of Jesus.

"Ye . . . killed the Prince of Life, whom God hath *raised from the dead;* whereof we are witnesses. And his name through faith in his name hath made this man strong . . . given him this perfect soundness in the presence of you all" (Acts iii, 15, 16). There is nothing like a mighty miracle of healing today for arresting the rotting confidence of the churches concerning even this fundamental of Christ's resurrection. When lifelong cripples suddenly leap into fullness of vigorous life, and blind eyes are suddenly opened in response to prayer, surely the most sceptical present knows that Jesus is **ALIVE**!

(e) To draw people within the sound of the gospel.

"And a great multitude followed him, because they saw his miracles which he did on them that were diseased" (John vi, 2). Let the reader trace out in the gospels this connection between crowds and healings. Is it not still, even apart from the chief aim of these Gifts in delivering the sick, a good thing to have crowds come within sound of the saving Word? Those who have been fortunate enough to see multitudes waiting for hours and hours outside great city halls, attracted by the grand news of sicknesses suddenly banished and infirmities miraculously cured—waiting to hear the simple evangelist proclaim the way of salvation—waiting eagerly for their turn to be healed of their diseases—these will have no doubt about the purpose of these Gifts in our day as well as in the Lord's! There is nothing so powerfully recommends Jesus the Saviour as Jesus the Healer! That is why in these awful days of increasing iniquity and satanic power every evangelist and missionary positively needs these Gifts of supernatural Healings to authenticate his heavenly message.

(f) To turn people to God.

This is even better than bringing them within sound of the gospel! It is the end of all true preaching and service. When Peter said to Aeneas, the eight-year-bed-ridden paralytic of

Lydda, "Christ Jesus maketh thee whole!" and when Aeneas immediately arose by the dynamic of that mightiest Name, "all that dwelt in Lydda and Saron saw him, and turned to the Lord." The inhabitants of a good town and its "county" saved *en masse* as the result of one gracious work of the Lord! Can such Gifts be lightly neglected in the face of the needs of today?

(g) To convince unbelievers of the truth of God's Word, mysterious though it may be.

"Believe me . . . or else believe me for the very works' sake," said Jesus, striving with all His gracious strength and argument to get men to believe for their temporal and eternal good. Present-day healings authenticate the Bible for those who have been taught to doubt it by modernistic blind guides. There are no miracles in modernism!

(h) To bring glory to God. Hallelujah!

"They were all amazed, and glorified God, saying, We never saw it on this fashion." "And all the people rejoiced for all the glorious things that were done by Him" (Mark ii, 12; Luke xiii, 17). Can the loudest critics of divine healing deny that the rejoicing of those who are suddenly loosed from palsy and spinal curvature and other hopeless diseases brings glory to our blessed Lord? And is there anywhere a people who praise God so continuously as those who believe in the Gifts of the Spirit? Or those who have been healed by the Lord?

(i) To inspire faith and courage in God's people.

As in their day the former servants of the Lord were enheartened in spite of surrounding scepticism, beholding the glorious triumph of their miracle-commission as the risen Lord worked continually with them still; so may His servants shout for joy today as they behold the working of the self-same commission under the Spirit's might, through these potent Gifts of Healings. JESUS IS ALIVE! is the trumpet voice of every miracle in our assemblies!

We must be content with this short list of Scripture uses of the Gifts, though the reader may search out many more for himself. And we must leave out altogether examples of divine healing through these Gifts today. Every Pentecostal assembly in the world, and there are thousands of them, will provide marvellous examples of incurable sicknesses and infirmities miraculously healed by the power of the Lord, either through the normal ministry of the assembly, or the visit of some simple evangelist equipped with these precious Gifts. Living examples of healing may be seen and heard in the testimony meetings of these assemblies. The reader is advised to go and see for himself the substantial and incontrovertible confirmation of these words.

With a few closing observations we must pass on to the next Gift.

Throughout this chapter the plural title of the Gifts of Healings has been emphasized. They are many, not one, as is generally supposed. A believer possessing one or more of them will be used of God in certain cases of sickness, but not necessarily in others. Some have great success in cases of blindness; some in deafness; some in cancer cases; some in internal disorders; some in fractures or distorted bones. The principle in all the Gifts is "as the Lord will."

The Gifts may operate by a touch or a word: in the latter case distance is no object (Psalm cvii, 20; Matt. viii, 8).

In exceptional cases healings may result from the operation of the Gifts *without* a word or a touch, by the very presence of the one possessed of them, as Peter, whose very shadow streamed forth like a mighty overflow of divine unction, sweeping all diseases before it (Acts v, 15); or from fabrics or garments which have been in contact with those possessed of the Gifts, as Paul at Ephesus (Acts xix, 12). What a gracious provision is this transmission of healing power for those at a distance from assemblies of believers!

Healing by anointing with oil (James v, 14) is not through the operation of these Gifts, but in response to obedience and in answer to believing prayer. In James it is the elders who are to anoint. In Mark vi, 13, Jesus' disciples also healed through anointing with oil. There is no authority for promiscuous anointing by men and women generally. But elders will not forget that their pastor is not only an elder with them, but that he is the presiding elder. This simple fact seems sometimes to be overlooked.

The laying on of hands as in Mark xvi, 18, is not limited to those possessing the Gifts of Healings. It is an act of faith for any "believer" as the context shows; for on the promise contained in it the Lord will graciously heal in response to living faith. The only condition here is "believing" (verse 17). While anointing with oil is for sick *believers* only, hands may be laid on the saved or the unsaved, providing the unsaved make request for prayer or are willing to be prayed for (John v, 6; vi, 37). The only question is "Wilt thou be made whole?" Indeed experience reveals the marvellous circumstance that sinners are more readily healed than saints! Which enforces what has been said under (e) above.

The power Jesus gave to the apostles and the seventy (Matt. x, 1; Luke x, 1) was not permanent (Matt. xvii, 16). It began to wane as Jesus was about to leave this world. I have discussed this in the early chapters of this book. But the Gifts of the Spirit are "without repentance." Even so they operate only as the Spirit wills, and there must be a response of active faith on the part of the sick one (Matt. ix, 22; xiii, 58).

Faith is positively necessary in the operation of these—or indeed any of the Gifts. It may be (1) substitutionary faith where the sick one is too feeble to believe for himself (Mark ii, 5); or (2) the faith of the sufferer alone (Matt. ix, 22); or (3) the faith of the minister alone in special circumstances such as coma or unconsciousness (Matt. ix, 25); or (4) the combined faith of sufferer and minister (Matt. ix, 28, 29). This last seems to be the most usual. But those who claim to possess the Gifts of Healings must personally shoulder the burden of faith and blame themselves, not the sufferer, for failure or only partial success. It is of course different with anointing and prayer and laying on of hands. Faith is the indispensable requisite in healings.

And from what has already been said it is clear that the Gifts do not work indiscriminately at the will of the possessor.

Not every blind man or deaf man or sick man can be healed at will by the Gifts. Bethesda's porches were filled with sick folk, all believers in divine healing, for they were all waiting for a heavenly miracle. And the Minister on this occasion was One supremely gifted with the power of the Spirit. Yet only one was actually healed—the one who actually got into touch with Jesus' living power. All *who really got into vital touch with the Lord,* however, were healed, not only on this occasion, but on every other occasion. It is not possible to state dogmatically why, among those who are prayed for today, some are healed and some are not. And certainly here is no room to discuss so large a problem. But here is a man who, it is quite certain, will never be healed, though he travel round all the assemblies and seek the ministrations of those most mightily endowed with divine power. He is desperately sick, and no doubt he has a Bible and believes. Ask him his name. It is Gehazi! His sickness shall cling to him so long as there is breath in his mortal body. For the Lord has decreed it. For we must remember that on the obverse side of divine healing is divine sickness (2 Kings v, 27).

But here are many others, all sick of a deadly sickness under God's corrective hand. Not one of them will ever be healed by all the expert *physicians* the ages could muster. Yet EVERY ONE MIGHT BE HEALED—in God's appointed way, a supernatural way; by the world called a foolish way. The way of the uplifted serpent of brass! The way of the Word of God (Num. xxi). There is healing by way of the Cross, brother — sister. Bring your sicknesses to Jesus!

We will not too greatly distress ourselves by asking how many stricken "Israelites" are today "seeking unto the physicians" instead of unto the Lord (2 Chron. xvi, 12). nor how many "Gehazis" walk into our meetings unrecognized. Neither will we make the mistake of Job's friends in supposing our sicknesses and others' are connected with personal sin. Neither let us, as those at Nazareth, and thousands today, prevent the operation of authentic Gifts by a heavy insulation of personal unbelief (Matt. xiii, 58). Rather let us seek the face of the Lord for Gifts and mightier Gifts and use them as He instructs, to make straight crooked little children, to set at ease tortured men and women and to turn the awful groans of the constant sufferer into shouts of joy and praise to our lovely delivering Jesus!

CHAPTER NINE

The Working of Miracles

... to another the working of miracles. 1 Cor. xii, 10.

THROUGH carelessness of thought and casualness in Scripture examination much mist has gathered round the really very precise word "miracle." The very richness and resilience of our English language has helped to increase the intensity of this mist. So that before we can clearly approach our study of the Working of Miracles, before we can even attempt a definition, we must take a careful look at the word "miracle" itself.

Many words we commonly employ have a precise and quite limited meaning. Many words, on the other hand, have many meanings, or many shades of meaning. Many words, again, through use and adaptation, have come to possess both this precise and this general application. The word "miracle" is one of them. Other words of the same sort that keep coming up in these studies are "faith," "prophecy," "discernment." We must carefully distinguish between this general and specific use of terms.

When we say that a certain sunset was a "miracle" of beauty or that a particular Christian is a "miracle" of grace, or that our mother is a "miracle" of patience, we are of course employing the word in a figurative sense, and in a general way that is not at all what is meant by the same word in the title of this chapter. When you say that the dawn sky was a "miracle" of loveliness you do not mean that there was anything more supernatural about it than about the most ordinary dawn that ever awoke the day. All you really mean is that it was a particularly beautiful sky; a particularly striking natural phenomenon. When you speak even of a "miracle" of grace you are not using the word in the same sense as in the title of this Gift. Though every conversion is a "miracle," as life itself is a "miracle," yet it is not a Miracle in the sense of dividing a stream by a sweep of a mantle or turning common dust into living insects with a gesture or making bread without flour or oven.

A conversion is a supernatural act in the spiritual realm; we do not call it a miracle. What we do call a miracle is a supernatural act on the natural plane. New-birth is really not more miraculous than birth, though one is spiritual and the other natural. To turn water into wine by the processes of nature, through the properties and growth of the vine, is if you like a natural "miracle." To turn water into wine by a sovereign act apart from the processes of nature is a Miracle in the meaning of the Spiritual Gift we are considering.

"Miracle" is a word used to denote this non-natural, beyond-natural, supernatural order of things. Those who refer to conversions as the "greater works" that the Lord promised are using the word "works" or "miracles" in this weaker figurative sense, a sense that the Lord did not intend at all. Jesus meant precisely literal MIRACLES, works contrary to nature, accomplishments, so to speak, of the impossible, sudden and unaccountable reversals of the order to which we are accustomed.

What makes it necessary to clear the ground with such platitudes as this is the fact that many intelligent and godly commentators, when they come to discuss miracles, tell us that the miracles accomplished by Christians today in fulfilment of Jesus' promise (John xiv, 12) are "miracles" of courage and zeal and reclamation. Such talk is to make of none effect the blessed Word of God and to discount every divine act that does not fall within the narrow limits of our poor human comprehension. If conversions are really the "greater works" promised by the Lord may we not reasonably demand to know where are the lesser works, such as opening blind eyes and raising the dead? It is an axiom that the greater includes the lesser.

A miracle, therefore, is a supernatural intervention in the ordinary course of nature; a temporary suspension of the accustomed order; an interruption of the system of nature as we know it. The Gift of the Working of Miracles operates by the energy or dynamic force of the Spirit in reversals or suspensions of natural laws. A miracle is a sovereign act of the Spirit of God irrespective of laws or systems. A miracle does not, as some cynical unbelievers say, demand the existence of an undiscovered law to explain it. A miracle has no explanation other than the sovereign power of the Lord. God is not bound by His own laws. God acts as He will either within or outside of what we understand to be laws, whether natural or supernatural. To speak of God as though He were circumscribed by the laws of His own making is to reduce Him to the creature plane and impair the very essence of His eternal attributes. When in a sudden and sovereign act God steps outside the circle by which His creatures or creation are boundaried we call it a miracle. And so does God in the Scriptures.

Then, further, the word Miracle in the meaning of this Gift refers exclusively to acts of Power. A miracle of knowledge is produced through the Word of Knowledge, and a miracle of wisdom is produced through the Word of Wisdom, as we have already seen. The Working of Miracles produces works of Power. And those who produce such works through this Gift are strikingly called by a word in the Greek that might be rendered as "miraclers," or perhaps better, "miraclers-of-miracles" (1 Cor. xii, 29).

And yet once more we must limit the meaning of the word Miracle, excluding even certain acts of power—those which have to do with the healing of the human body—and including only those which concern the laws of inanimate nature or the miraculous manipulation of objects—turning water into wine, bringing fire from heaven, opening the sea, stilling the tempest, and so forth. Miracles of healing are wrought not through the Gift of the Working of Miracles but through the Gifts of Healings. I know some hold that sicknesses of the body come under the Gifts of Healings for correction, but that deformities and fractures come within the province of the Working of Miracles. This, I submit, leads to much confusion. It seems far more consistent to regard all maladies of the human frame, whether diseases or deformities, as within the beneficient reach of the Gifts of Healings, and all other miracles of power (excluding some we shall notice in the next chapter) as within the scope of the Working of Miracles. Note the distinction between "miracles" and "gifts of healings" in 1 Corinthians xii, 28.

"What is the use of miracles?" we sometimes hear—a question usually associated with cynics and busybodies, who merely want to fortify their pet obstructions and resistances; a question, therefore, which can often be ignored. But if there are those who sincerely wish to learn the answer to such an elementary question it will be found written large all over God's most precious Word. Let us consider some Scripture uses of the Gift:

(a) The Gift was used for the miraculous deliverance of God's people out of the hand of the enemy (Exodus xiv, 16).

Millions of men and women and children with their flocks and herds encamped beside the sea. Liberated! Compassed about with songs of deliverance . . . Look! A cloud of dust to the west. A mist of shimmering light. The hot sun glancing on a myriad spears, gleaming on a thousand chariots and a sea of burnished helmets. The Egyptian host! Trapped. The impassable sea. The inescapable foe. Helplessness and hopelessness. The people's cry of despair. Even Moses complains . . . Then Jehovah speaks. A lifted rod. The swirl and heave of waters. What ailest thou, O sea, that thou fleest? Consternation for triumph in one host; victory for dismay in the other! The camp moves through the congealed waters. The floods stand upright as a heap. The host pass as on dry land. The enemy said, I will pursue. Thou didst blow with thy wind, the sea covered them; they sank as lead in the mighty waters. Who is like unto Thee . . . doing wonders!

Is Jehovah's arm paralysed—His mighty breath

exhausted—that He cannot deliver by a miracle as of old? Are there not countless stories of His servants' supernatural deliverances from certain destruction in these our days? Does God stop no trains, direct no cars, deflect no hurricanes, prevent no fires, muzzle no beasts, disperse no lightnings, still no tempests NOW for his people's deliverance? "Then forward still, 'tis Jehovah's will, though the billows dash and spray. With a conquering tread we will push ahead; He'll roll the seas away!"

(b) To provide for those in want.

God has His controlling hand upon men through their natural desires. Thirst is a grand thing if it turns us to the Living Fountain of Waters. It is terrible if it turns us in anger against our leaders. For human anger is indeed a dry and thirsty land where no water is.

Multitudes athirst in Rephidim. No well nor spring nor stream nor smallest rivulet anywhere. Except in the heavens where they forgot to look. The intensified misery of murmuring. Even the little children caught the discontent from their elders and piped it out like music out of tune. Murmuring grows to violence. These stones! Why not be rid of our helpless leader! The Lord is not among us . . . What shall Moses do? Jehovah speaks. The rod again. He opened the rock, and the waters gushed out; they ran in the dry places like a river. He gave them drink as out of the great depths. Hallelujah! We have remembered that God is our Rock. Jesus! Living Fount of Water of Life. Out of Horeb's legal flint there streams Grace enough to quench the killing thirst of every Jehovah-offending sinner. Our Blessed Rock is a standing water. Sinai's riven Rock has become a fountain of waters (Exodus xvii).

Shall any say that our Jesus is not able today to give water to the thirsty even in the most impossible circumstances? Thirsty one—in Sahara's choking sand or sin's parching desert— Jesus stands upon the rock with uplifted hands for thee. Ask Him. Thou canst not do less. He requireth no more! Bless His Name!

The cupboard is empty. Bare as the barrel in Sarepta. All is

111

well. Do the Lord's bidding. Dip with faith's miracle-measure. According to that measure it shall still be done unto you. The barrel shall not waste today for the simple BELIEVER. Elijah is ascended. Jesus is risen! He is for you. Where the age of faith is not past the age of miracles is not past.

The need of one is nothing to Him who thinks in ones and dispenses in billions. "Can He give bread also?" is the voice of unbelief that comes to us as a legacy from the faithless believers of old (Psalm lxxviii, 20). Yes, Bread and water; both sure. Well-water and Living Water. Meal-bread and Living Bread. Do we not catch the echo of age-old unbelief?—"Can He *still* work miracles?"

Make them sit down. In order and decency. What is there in store? Nothing—save this handful. It is enough in the hands of Omnipotence. What is enough for one is enough for Jesus. A multitude to Him is only a succession of ones, all dearly loved. Yes, you say; it is spiritual bread the Lord supplies today. That is only the application, I reply. The sermon itself was preached in terms of empty stomachs and baker's bread. So today. There are thousands of empty stomachs as well as hungry hearts. But the crowds are not following Jesus. They have been "sent away" by the church to buy pitiful "pennyworths" of sorrow and emptiness in the "villages" of the godless world (Mark vi, 36, 37).

The godless, not the saints, have got the Saviour's bread, while there are basketsful of over-supply for the Whosoever-will-nots dying in the midst of plenty, cursing for bread.

There is a little company of God's people striving to lead the hungry up to the mount again to the Lord, where through the Gifts of the Spirit they may have bread. The remainder of Christendom is driving them down the mount, away from the Lord, into the world for their needs. The "church" has sent the sick to the world, the hungry to the world, the seeker after truth to the world, the seeker after happiness to the world. It is finishing the last days before the Coming of the Mighty Reckoner by sending the seeking sinner to the world—and often to the devil.

Devoted followers of the Lord, "Give ye them to eat." Christ's crucified hands are still creative hands. On the shores of Tiberias after resurrection He stood unknown in His accustomed might and made bread for the hungry (John xxi, 9).

"Send them away," says Christendom still, where need is concerned. "Give ye them to eat," says Christ still. Baken bread and Bread of Life. Calvary's portion is enough ALL. Five bleeding wounds: Love-broken, God-given, Christ-blest Bread. Less than Calvary is not enough for *one* poor hungry body or soul.

(c) To carry out divine judgments and disciplines.

For God's power operates both ways: in encouragement and restraint. No man ever enjoyed more mighty evidence of the reality of the Living God than Pharaoh. No man ever had more opportunity of repentance. Before God destroyed him for his wicked obduracy He gave him the most astonishing display of miracle signs that the Bible contains. By a sweep of the rod of Moses the rivers and waters of Egypt ran blood, producing death and evil odour. By another sweep the same rivers, become water once more, grew prolific in revolting life—frogs. By a third divine stroke the very dust under the people's feet leapt into crawling insect life filling the land. By another the air they breathed bred swarms of hateful flies. Then the cattle they used and bartered and ate fell stricken with grievous disease. Foul boils and sores issued from the ash of their cooking stoves. Driving fire and smiting hail hurtled out of the fruitful clouds. Devouring locusts and caterpillars came out of the land they cultivated. Black darkness fell out of the source of light. Death — out of the fountain of life. A series of Miracles redoubled in their reversal in each case. All — excepting perhaps the last -- by the miracle-power and authority with which the great Jehovah had invested His meek servant Moses. Every one leaving the Children of Israel without hurt or annoy.

The same power which at the word of a sanctified and Spirit-filled fisherman centuries later slew two who had without provocation attempted to deceive the Holy Spirit of God (Acts v). The same power which today ... But let me repeat a story out of Mr. Burton's thrilling new book that every Christian in the world should read —*God Working With Them.*

On the shores of Lake Kisali in Mr. Hodgson's section of the Congo Evangelistic Mission, of which Mr. Burton is chief, the swindling witch-doctors were troubling the simple Gospel preachers. They threatened to annihilate the families of believers attending the mission meetings. Without avail. Then they schemed to destroy the evangelists. As a native evangelist was returning from preaching one evening he found that sorcerers had been taking scrapings from his bed and threads from his Sunday coat, to "bewitch" him. "At last," shouted the chief sorcerer triumphantly as he was discovered in his evil work, "we have all that is necessary to bring about your end. You will fall dead at sunrise tomorrow morning."

"Next morning," Mr. Burton proceeds, "a big crowd gathered about the door of the evangelist's hut to see if the magic of the witch-doctor could accomplish what he boasted.

Just at sunrise the evangelist opened his door, and went to beat the drum for the sunrise prayer meeting, when there was an awful cry at the far end of the village, where the sorcerer himself, on coming out of his hut, suddenly threw his arms into the air with a shriek of agony, and fell back dead."

Should not this one story enhearten every believer in every movement to seek earnestly the power of the Lord that the Word might be confirmed according to promise and that Satan's determined emissaries might be openly discomfited?

Authority is given to the servant of the Lord in the Gifts of the Spirit. Authority to ensure the will of the Most High, either with the concurrence of the people or despite their organized resistance.

(d) To confirm the preached Word (Acts xiii, 11, 12).

After the beloved and learned deputy of Cyprus in his earnest search for truth had admitted into his society the subtle Elymas, no doubt impressed by his satanic miracles of imposture, he was astounded one day to hear the message of three newly arrived missionaries. A message of One Jesus. Which was true—the message of the sorcerer or of the missionaries? Elymas used his powerful magic to turn away the seeker from the Lord, Paul, moved to the depths, filled with the Holy Ghost and His conquering Gifts, left the evil-doer in total darkness for a season, blinded. "Then the deputy, when he SAW WHAT WAS DONE, believed, being astonished at the doctrine of the Lord." A miracle settles every quarrel concerning the authority of the Gospel message.

(e) To deliver in unavoidable situations of danger (Matt. viii, 23).

Sometimes the most cautious Christian in the course of the most ordinary duties finds himself in a position of great peril. The fisherman's life is typical. Storms will arise and overwhelm the stoutest barque. But a miracle such as the ever blessed Carpenter's will still bring out of their distresses those who are at their wits' end. Sometimes a miracle is God's only way out for us! Thrice unhappy at such times those who do not believe in them!

(f) To raise the dead.

We will discuss this when we come to it in the Gift of Faith.

(g) To display God's power and magnificence.

The evidential character of all miracles is strongly emphasized throughout the Scriptures. "Praise Him for His mighty acts"; they show forth "His excellent greatness!" Jesus' miracles established His Messiahship for the imprisoned Baptist (Matt. xi, 5); they were a greater witness to His divine authority than the words of the mightiest prophets (John v, 36; x, 25); and a stronger recommendation of His divine claims than even His own authoritative words (John v, 38).

In the original (see Young) miracles are called "powers," meaning explosions of almightiness; "wonders," impelling staggering astonishment; "works," the expected expression of the Divine walking among men; and "signs," "the visible tokens of an invisible power," for every miracle is not only a power and a wonder in itself; it is a sign of something else.

Like a red sunset: not only a wonder in itself, but a sign of a fine day tomorrow. Jesus' miracles were a sign that He was verily God alive among men. His continued miracles today are repeated signs that He is still ALIVE among men!

But remember that when the miracles of our Lord are referred to today, the thought is usually of His miracles of healing (Acts iv, 22). These, as we have seen, are not the work of the Gift we are considering but of the Gifts of Healings. Once more we must bear in mind for clarity's sake that every operation of every one of the Nine Gifts is a miracle; a miracle, that is, in its own particular order.

Then though God graciously condescends to employ human agents in His miraculous works, which is the very meaning of the Gifts of the Spirit, He can, of course, and does, work miracles entirely without human intervention; as Babel's confusion of tongues, Sodom's "vengeance of fire," "the fiery, cloudy pillar," the "common bush ablaze with God," the star that traced a bright way to Bethlehem, the blinding light that illumined Moses' astonished face.

And in some miracles angels and cherubim are the agents, as Siloam's troubled pool, Zacharias' dumbness, the slaying of the Egyptian firstborn. Who hinders God's hosts doing His pleasure today?

And some miracles produce effects so similar to nature's that they are sometimes quite innocently, because ignorantly, passed over as merely natural happenings. The force that calmed the raging tempest on that memorable trip to Tarshish was not the sudden change in meteorological conditions but the ejected body of the disobedient prophet (Jonah i and ii). The uninitiated crew of a following ship might just have added under the day's date an entry in the log book: "Wind—sudden change from N.E. to S.W. by W." So today. We can drink a cup of choicest miracle-wine without knowing that it never knew the branch of the vine nor the rigours of the wine-press (John ii, 9); only the touch of a Saviour's blessed hands!

Perhaps if we were to heave overboard, like the inspired sailors of old, our disgruntled humours and disobedient tempers into the turbulent waters of our constant distresses, Jehovah would work an immediate miracle for us! And if the "church" would throw overboard even now her wilful and disobedient modernistic "prophets" she might emerge from the billows that have well-nigh engulfed her: and perhaps the "prophets" themselves by infinite grace be "vomited out" repentant, regenerated, changed and happy men.

Was it not last week (16/3/34) we read in the papers that the scientists had attributed the recent earthquake in India to "underloading of the earth's crust"? What if its cause was rather that same overloading of earth's sin that shook the earth with judgment convulsions when God's gentle Son gave forth His life upon a Roman gibbet! (Matt. xxvii, 51).

And finally, though all miracles are parables of life, they must neither be naturalized away nor spiritualized away. Beware of the repeated modern attempts, even among those who are born again, to attenuate or extinguish the miraculous. These are Satan's devices. A few years ago an expedition left for the desert of Sinai to find out what exactly the manna was upon which the old Israelites subsisted for so long! They "discovered" it in the gum exuding from a certain shrub! A glance at an ancient Manuscript would have told them that "the manna CEASED" on the day following the crossing of Jordan! (Joshua v, 12).

All the "proofs" of all the happenings in the Bible are for the believer in the Record Itself. The proof of the Flood for us is not in the geologists' sample bottles (God bless them if they have discovered God's Word to be true—even with a pick and a hammer; and may some inspired scientist send a consignment of such picks and hammers to our "theological" colleges to replace the penknives and braziers with which, like Jehoiakim, they are destroying the precious Word of the Lord, and more-over therewith "this land" of ours!—Jer, xxxvi, 23, 29)—our sufficient proofs are in the chapters of Genesis. And remember that when you have succeeded in finding a whale that could swallow Jonah and a Jonah capable of living for days and nights in a monster's interior you have not establi

117

the miracle: you have extinguished it.

Neither, spiritualizing, must we spiritualize the miracles away. Yes, praise God, He gives spiritual sight. But that, though the best, is not all. He gives physical eyesight to the blind. And the best sermon on spiritual blindness is still a miracle of physical sight-giving. So with all the other miracles. And as we sing the old salvation hymns based on miracles of healing let us by grace expel the unctuous unbelief the centuries have imported into them, and really believe that the sick that met with divers pains on that blessed Capernaum eventide really went away with joy without their physical pains, as a prophecy to those who are in pain today. And let us still believe according to Hebrews thirteen, eight, that Jesus Christ is the same yesterday, and today, and for ever, that His touch has still its ancient power, and that He can really today hear, and in mercy, through the blessed Gifts of the Spirit, really heal us all.

CHAPTER TEN

The Gift of Faith

. . .to another faith. 1 Cor. xii, 9.

Faith is doubtless the greatest of the three Gifts of Power. Faith is one of the wonderful things of the Bible. It blossomed for a season in the scented walks of Paradise. Its perfect blooms are found on the steeps of Patmos. From Paradise to Patmos it marks the trail of the company of the blessed, the heaven-bound, happy-hearted Pleasers of God.

We must scrutinize this wonderful word narrowly, even more closely than the word "miracle" in the last chapter, if we are to find out its exact meaning here. For it not only has like "miracle" and prophecy" and other words a specific and a general signification; it has several specific meanings; these it will be useful at once to review and compare.

The Gift of Faith is distinct from saving faith (Acts xvi, 31). Saving faith goes before salvation; the Gift of Faith can only be received after salvation. True, saving faith is itself a gift of God (Eph. ii, 8), the gift of God to the sinner that he might receive Jesus. The Gift of Faith is a gift of the Spirit to the saint that he might work miracles, or rather receive them. The Gift of Faith is miraculous like all the other gifts of the Spirit. Saving faith is divine, but not miraculous in the narrow sense discussed in the last chapter. Saving faith issues according to expected plan in the fulfilment of promises concerning salavtion. Miracle-Faith issues in unexpected things— or things that only Faith expects.

Under this head we might add that there is a natural faith, as there is a natural wisdom, quite distinct from every form of divine faith whether miraculous or non-miraculous. Natural

119

faith is that which, say, the farmer exercises when he sows his seed: "the husbandman waiteth for the precious fruit of the earth." Faith in history— believing a record—by which alone we are assured, say, that Queen Elizabeth lived and reigned, is also natural faith. It does not save, even when it receives the facts of Jesus' life and death. It is a head thing: faith is of the heart. Believing the record that God gave of His Son (1 John v, 10) means not only nodding mental assent, but committing ourselves to all its implications. Devils have head faith in perfection. They believe and tremble. They have a conviction amounting to postive certainty concerning the things that unbelievers reject: that is why they tremble. That men should doubt facts about Jesus that devils believe is the result of devil's work in the heart. Devils do not cast doubt on things they do not believe but on things they do. They insult the God they respect and traduce in human hearing the Sovereignty they must acknowledge. This is what constitutes the fight of *faith*. The adversary for his own ends makes it difficult for us to believe what he thoroughly believes himself—what, for his work in our hearts, disposed by sin to listen to him, would be perfectly obvious truths. The modernists have succumbed to his devices. The Lord give us victory in the fight.

The Gift of Faith is distinct from Faith the Fruit of the Spirit (Gal. v, 22). Faith is significantly the only one that is both in the Galatian list of Fruits and the Corinthian list of Gifts. Faith the Fruit is for character; Faith the Gift is for power. Those children of God who have Faith the Fruit of the Spirit believe God in such a way that they are assured of salvation, and believe His Word in such a way that they obey His commands; but those who possess Faith the Gift of the Spirit believe God in such a way that God honours their word as His own and miraculously brings it to pass. "He shall have whatsoever he *saith*" (Mark xi, 23); "Thou shalt also decree a thing, and it shall be established unto thee" (Job xxii, 28); "There shall not be dew nor rain these years, but according to *my* word"—"And it rained not on the earth by the space of three years and six months" (1 Kings xvii, 1;

James v, 17; 2 Kings ii, 22).

Saving Faith goes before salvation; Faith the Fruit comes after salvation; Faith the Gift comes after the baptism in the Holy Spirit.

The Gift of Faith is distinct from the Working of Miracles, though both produce miracles. Miracles' operation is more active than passive: Faith's operation is more passive than active. Miracles' power *does* things by the Spirit: Faith's power receives or enjoys things by the Spirit. If Daniel in the lions' den had slain the dreaded beasts with a gesture it would have been a miracle wrought by the Working of Miracles. That he rested unharmed in the presence of the fully active beasts was a miracle wrought through the Gift of Faith. The Working of Miracles employs active faith that actively works a miracle. The Gift of Faith employs active faith that passively expects a miracle, a sustained or continuous miracle. If the disciples in the tempest-tossed boat had remained calmly assured in spite of the roaring and the turbulence of wind and wave the Lord would have shown them a Miracle of Faith, taking them through the billows as though they did not exist. Since He could not get them to trust Him *in* the storm He was compelled to remove it by a lesser miracle of the Working of Miracles. Since He could not pacify their hearts in the fury of the tempest He had to pacify them by pacifying the waters. Since He failed to get them to *believe* for the peace and security they could not see He had to *show* them peace and safety to calm their fears. That is the difference between a miracle of the Gift of Miracles and a miracle of the Gift of Faith.

And of course the Gift of Faith is distinct from the Gifts of Healings, All miracles of healing are wrought by the Gifts of Healings, through what we might call *general faith.* The Gift of Faith produces other miracles which we will consider in a moment.

Having thus cleared the ground we are in a good enough position for our definition.

The Gift of Faith is a supernatural endowment by the Spirit

whereby that which is uttered or desired by man, or spoken by God, shall eventually come to pass. This human or divine miracle-utterance, or miracle-assurance, covers blessing or cursing, creation or destruction, removal or alteration. It is different from the Working of Miracles and the Gifts of Healings in that often its operations are not immediately or even generally observable. The operation of Miracles is more of an act, as when the waters were opened by Moses or Elijah; while the operation of the Gift of Faith is more of a process, as when Isaac blessed Jacob, in terms which could only be fulfilled over a long period of time (Gen. xxvii, 27; Heb. xi, 20). Faith the Gift is equally miraculous with all the other Gifts, but we might say that its power or manifestation is of greater duration than those of the Gifts of Miracles or Healings.

The Gift of Faith is erroneously regarded as the basis of all the other Gifts of the Spirit. This is to confuse the different kinds of faith. Faith (what I have above called "general faith") is certainly necessary to the operation of all the Gifts, even the operation of the Gift of Faith; but the Gift of Faith is a supernatural endowment quite distinct from this "general faith," and equally distinct from the other eight supernatural endowments of the Spirit. All the Nine Gifts operate by faith, even the great Gift of Faith; just as all motor-cars run on petrol, even those great six- wheeled motor petrol-tanks.

What is that faith that operates the Gifts and underlies everything in the Christian life from newbirth to full redemption in the glory? It is that "general faith," the gift of God which as a seed saves, and which as a fruit both enjoys and pleases God, here and for ever.

Perhaps we shall understand this a little better if we examine still more closely the relationship between saving faith, faith the fruit, and faith the gift of the Spirit. Now the possession of saving faith precedes but does not guarantee the possession of Faith the Fruit. Faith germinates and grows— "from faith to faith" (Romans i, 17). Saving faith is as the Seed. The seed will produce, say, a fig tree, which may be with or without fruit or much fruit. You may have the Gift without the Fruit or without much Fruit, but not without the Seed. The Seed will, if you foster it, produce the Fruit, but it will not produce the Gift. You may have the Fruit without the Gift, but again not without the Seed. The Fruit comes from the Seed—the Gift direct from the hands of the Lord by the Holy Spirit. The Gift certainly does not include the Fruit nor the Fruit the Gift, yet the more of the Fruit we have the better the Gift will work—which, however, is true of all the Nine Gifts. Fruit does not work miracles, not even *Faith* the Fruit. But Faith the Fruit *works* Faith the Gift, and all the other Gifts as well. Faith the Gift is a dormant Gift without Faith the Fruit.

The Gift of Faith does not include nor substitute nor swamp all other faith. It is not as though the Gift of Faith made it impossible for its possessor to doubt God any more. The possessor of the Gift finds it no less an effort of consecration and will to believe God in ordinary things (non-miraculous things) than any other Christian. And the Gift of Faith does not, so to speak, make a man fool-proof for heaven. Miracle Faith does not fit a man for heaven any more than Miracle-Speaking-with-Other Tongues. It serves, like all the other Gifts, God's temporary ends till that which is perfect is come. The things of divine character that fit us for heaven are the province of the Fruit-Faith. The Gift-Faith is for heavenly miracles this side of heaven. Faith the Fruit, producing the wine of character, grows on the branch abiding in the Vine. Faith the Gift at the Master's bidding "Draw out now" pours miracle-wine by the Spirit direct from human waterpots. Heavenly miracles this side of heaven! There is a Faith that projects beyond the Gates into the eternal realm. "Now abideth Faith." It is the perfected Fruit handling the perfected Gift, now no longer "a child" but developed into the stature of a full grown man. This we pondered under 1 Corinthians XIII, 13, in Chapter Seven.

Shall we follow our usual plan and consider some Scripture uses of the Gift?

(a) The Gift of Faith was employed for direct supernatural blessing in fulfilment of human utterance.

Old Isaac, bent with age, half blind with the years, misguided by parental favouritism, deceived by a scheming wife who in his handsome youth came from far for the love of him, for all the weakness of human ambition and all the intricacy of human expediency now reaches forth groping hands and pronounces Jacob's blessing, not upon Esau as he thought, but upon Jacob, according to mighty divine plan! Who can circumvent the Almighty? Whom God designs to bless shall be blessed, though subtlety's self intervene to divert the blessing. "See, the smell of my son is as the smell of a field which the Lord *hath* blessed: therefore God give thee of the dew of heaven, and the fatness of the earth, and plenty of corn and wine: let the people serve thee, and the nations bow down to thee: be lord over thy brethren, and let thy mother's sons bow down to thee, " Thus "by faith Isaac blessed Jacob concerning things *to come*" (Gen. xxvii, 28; Heb. xi, 20), inerrantly and assuredly delivering his words, charged with divine breath, and the irresistible dynamic of Miracle-Faith, and trusting in full assurance of faith that the years would see under God's hands the certain fulfilment of them, while he slept in Mamre's cave with Abraham and Sarah, awaiting with us the coming of the Faithful Fulfiller of the very words of those who dare to trust Him. "Whosoever shall say . . . .and shall not doubt . . . but shall believe . . . he shall have whatsoever he saith." By faith also Jacob, when he was a-dying, pronounced blessings over Ephraim and Manasseh, and blessings and cursings over the heads of his own sons, in terms that Jehovah must hear and bring to pass, for He is sworn to honour the fiat of Faith as His own creative Word.

What about the two-finger benedictions and maledictions of popery? Breath is not benediction; gesticulation is not faith. Only "what the Lord hath spoken . . . will He make good," and "the curse causeless shall not come" (Num. xxiii, 19; Prov. xxvi, 2). Hierarchy may pronounce, but who shall "bring it to pass"! God is not behind the pomp of priestcraft. He is behind

Faith. Faith only can bless—or unbless. Praise God. "He hath blessed and I cannot reverse it." "How can I curse whom God hath not cursed?" (Num. xxiii, 8, 20). The anathemas of the cunning, God shall turn, like Saul's sword, into their own bowels.

(b) For personal protection in perilous circumstances.

Political jealousy may seal "the mouth of the den" where the servant of God lies in the midst of ravenous beasts, but Faith unseals the den and "stops the mouths of lions" instead, because the humble prophet "believes in his God" (Daniel vi, 17, 23; Heb. xi, 33). The passions of hell are muzzled where the simple child of God looks calmly to the promises of heaven. Guilt cries "with a lamentable voice" while "innocency," worshipping, enjoys mighty peace in peril through the power of the Gifts of the Spirit. And what terror of wild beasts has he who, like the tempted Lord, believes "there shall no evil befall thee" (Mark i, 13)? Or what fear of adders' venom for him who, like Paul, trusts that in the Name of Jehovah they shall tread upon the adder, and in the Name of Jesus they shall take up serpents (Mark xvi, 18; Acts xxviii, 5)?

What a wonderful Gift is this for the missionary who must sometimes encounter snarling leopards and crouching tigers and prowling lions and lurking serpents! Cartridges (though I have no word against them; perhaps they are the legitimate descendants of good Scriptural arrows) are a poor substitute for Faith. Cartridges prove nothing. Faith proves GOD.

And are not the murderous passions of envious men more terrible than the talons of dragons and the fangs of cobras? What unimaginable force lies hidden in the simple record, "He passing through the midst of them went His way" (Luke iv, 30)! Defeat by miraculous evasion is even more mighty than defeat by heaven-aided conflict; for it embroils us in no dangerous intrigue and exalts us in no proud personal exploit.

(c) For supernatural sustenance in famine or fasting.

The bits that drop from heaven by the beaks of carrion birds are sweeter than the delicacies of the king's table—especially if, like Ahab, the king is away from God. Such bits of bread and flesh interpret the mysteries of earth's dearth and heaven's fullness. When by the precious Gifts of the Spirit you have proved God thus for *yourself* you can speak authoritative words to empty meal barrels and their insentient staves must in the Name of the Lord fulfil your bidding for somebody else. When by the river of death you have found life and food for a year for yourself you can go to the chamber of death and restore the dead to the sorrowing mother (1 Kings xvii, 3, 4, 23).

Fear turned poor Elijah, after all *that,* into a craven fugitive. And many a poor little "Elijah" since. He went "a day's journey" out of the will of God. Juniper trees do not bear food. But, blessed be God, angels do. Even for recreant failures. The residue of real Faith keeps active in periods of relative unbelief. Hallelujah! Angel's portions eaten with Faith will yield sustenance for forty days and nights, as in Horeb (1 Kings xix, 4-8), and the Word of God alone, if assimilated by this same Miracle-Faith, will support for a like period, as in the wilderness of Judea (Matt. iv). But let those who look longingly at these marvellous records of fasting be warned that what faith most of us have will consort far better with feasting than with fasting, and if to fulfil all righteousness we wish to fast let us do so as Daniel did, fasting not from food, but from pleasant food. Faith supports; fanaticism destroys—destroys even the faith it purports to demonstrate.

Faith seems to be especially the Gift that covers God's servants in positions of unavoidable danger and distress. Danger from starvation, beasts, elements (fire, water), war, unseen powers. Faith calmly faces peril while God supports— or extricates.

And if there are those who feel that "all this sort of thing is past," let them read again how George Muller of the Bristol Orphanages, with hundreds of hungry children, and positively empty larders, prayed God's blessing upon bare cups and platters, and as he prayed, churns of milk came in at one door and baskets of bread at another, till plenty filled the hungry mouths and joy the happy hearts.

(d) For receiving the astounding promises of God.

Faith, rooted deep in God, ignores the years and human weakness and cries a loud Amen to staggering promises. "And Abraham was an hundred years old when his son Isaac was born unto him" in his goodly tent in Gerar. "He staggered not at the promise . . . but was strong in faith, giving glory to God" (Gen. xxi, 5; Rom. iv, 20). Twenty-five years—fifty—will not suffice to reduce the power of a mighty promise when like a living seed it reposes in the living soil of Faith. Faith's Amen really fulfils every promise in advance. It is only human Nays and Buts that destroy the Yeas in God's precious promises.

(e) For administering spiritual correction to gross offenders.

Concerning an unrepentant offender among the saints of Corinth Paul instructs in a Faith that enforces the carrying out of his judgment. "In the Name of our Lord Jesus Christ, when ye are gathered together, and my spirit, with the power of our Lord Jesus Christ, to deliver such an one unto Satan for the destruction of the flesh, that the spirit may be saved in the day of the Lord Jesus." For the supernatural hand of the Lord is disciplinary and punitive as well as encouraging and delivering. An echo comes out of the long past here and we recall those "youths" who were destroyed by wild beasts as punishment for their unprovoked and blasphemous mockery of Elisha after the translation of his teacher Elijah (2 Kings ii, 23, 24). Through the Gifts of the Spirit God's restraining hand is still on obstinate blasphemers and dangerous rebels.

(f) For supernatural victory in the fight (Ex. xvii, 11).

The world's hosts can never prevail against the people of God while His servants are holding up holy hands to Him, filled with victorious Miracle-Faith. And let critics of the Gifts notice the precious efficacy of *helping* Faith in this record. There would be more victorious miracles today if instead of cynically triumphing over the lack of them, the Church provided more Aarons and Hurs to hold up Moses' hands in our upper-room "Rephidims." The Lord is still our victorious War-Flag, our triumphant Battle-Standard, "Jehovah Nissi"! Pentecost would be still more effective with helping faith from others.

127

(g) To assist in domestic and industrial problems.

In these days of industrial depression, what a boon to the people of God would be men filled with the Gifts of the Spirit! What can a poor woman do when her husband is dead and creditors are pressing to take away her sons as slaves, to foot the heavy bills? One pot of oil and "empty vessels not a few" – and by the power of the Spirit there arises a miraculous little business sufficient to silence the creditors and satisfy the needs of the happy family. How far have the God-forgetting nations drifted from heaven's solution to world problems! Can the experiments of politicians, however wise, really compare in such an emergency with the solutions of an all-wise God? Let the people of God at least believe that He is still able to step supernaturally down into the need and miraculously supply it for His own (2 Kings iv, 1-7).

(h) To raise the dead.

This instance we agreed to carry over from our study of the Working of Miracles. To go back to the figure of the spectrum that we employed early in this book we must remember that the Gifts of the Spirit are really an analysis of the sum of the wisdom and the power of the most holy God. And just as the blue and the green in the prismatic analysis do not really subsist apart from one another, though they may be distinguished in a general way for examination, so the Gifts of the Spirit, though we may consider them apart, are really one graded and indivisible expression of the fullness of God's infinite ability. In the mighty act of raising the dead Lazarus or Dorcas we shall doubtless find that all the Gifts of Power are employed in combination, including even Gifts of Revelation and Inspiration. We have said that the Working of Miracles *works* miracles, while the Gift of Faith trusts for *miracles*. Both operations are here. That Lazarus came forth at all is an operation of Miracle-Faith. That he came forth bound is an operation of the Gift of Miracles. And that he came forth well, and not sick of the disease of which he died, is of course due to the Gifts of Healings.

This overlapping of the Gifts is wonderful to think about. That sometimes there seems real difficulty in ascribing the appropriate Gift to certain instances is due to this marvellous overlapping. Sometimes we cannot dogmatically say whether we are beholding a miracle of knowledge or a miracle of power. In Matthew xvii, 27, for instance, did Jesus know the coin was in the fish's mouth, or did He put it there? Perhaps there was a combination of both. This is interesting but not really important, for the miracle remains the same in any case.

And in Jacob's blessings and cursings considered above at (a), did he by a Word of Wisdom learn the future, or by Miracle-Faith determine it? Or both? I have included it under the Gift of Faith because I am convinced that Faith positively determined the future (in harmony of course with God's mysterious foreordination) as Jacob, clothed with the Spirit's anointing, pronounced the words. Even as the words of a greater than Jacob determined the destiny of a certain fig tree on the slopes of Olivet.

(i) Finally Faith is the Gift employed in casting out evil spirits.

Jesus, we have seen, rebuked the evil spirits, or cast them out with His Word, trusting His Father to honour that anointed rebuke or Word by delivering. A sudden deliverance from demons by the use of Spirit-filled, prayer-soaked fabrics as in Acts xix, 12, is likewise brought about by this Gift of Faith. Sufferers from hopeless depression of spirit and sleeplessness, the work not of disease but of evil powers, can be delivered by this beneficent Gift.

The present-day uses of the Gift are exactly the same as those above. For protection or deliverance from storm lightning, shipwreck, evil men, evil spirits, wild beasts, pestilence, calamity; for triumph over every evil power and supernatural protection in all circumstances. Is the command to covet earnestly the best Gifts a futile one?

We must run quickly to a conclusion in our study of this most mighty Gift. Faith's operation is less spectacular than that of any other Gift. It is manifested often secretly, silently, over long periods, but none the less surely and miraculously.

Jesus says, "Have faith in God" (Mark xi, 22). Nothing

could be more miraculous than the faith described in this context. Does not this give us authority for expecting that any ordinary Christian may at the will of the Spirit be equipped with these greater Gifts? Removing mountains (literal mountains), withering and uprooting trees, casting out demons, are miracles especially associated with this wonderful Gift (Mark xi, 20, 22; Luke xvii, 6; Matt. xvii, 20, 21). And obviously the faith mentioned in 1 Corinthians xiii, 2, is this Miracle-Gift of Faith, as the Knowledge, Wisdom, Tongues and Prophecy in the same chapter are also the supernatural Gifts.

And though the Gift is not the basis of the other Gifts it may often operate in conjunction with others, as we have seen. The probable combination of Gifts necessary for the fulfilment of the divine commission in Matthew x, 8, is as follows:

1. Heal the sick (ordinary sickness)—(GIFTS OF HEALINGS).
2. Cleanse the lepers (incurable sickness, Infirmities, afflictions and cripples come under the same head)—(GIFTS OF HEALINGS).
3. Cast out demons—(DISCERNING OF SPIRITS AND FAITH).
4. Raise the dead—(FAITH, WORKING OF MIRACLES AND GIFTS OF HEALINGS).

We shall return to this subject of the combination of Gifts in subsequent chapters.

The Faith of Hebrews Eleven, that present assurance of future certainties and invisable realities, is principally this marvellous Miracle-Faith; but all other kinds of faith discussed in this study appear in the chapter; saving faith in verse 31 illustratively); faith the fruit in verses 4, 13, 26, 36; and what I have called "general faith," including saving, sanctifying, and all blessing-receiving, God-pleasing, heaven-inheriting faith, underlying even Miracle-Faith, in verses 3 and 6.

Once more I ask, Is it in vanity or mockery that the command still rings out from the infallible, immutable Word: Desire Spiritual Gifts . . .?

CHAPTER ELEVEN

Speaking with Tongues

. . . to another divers kinds of tongues. 1 Cor. xii, 10.

THE remaining three related Gifts of the Spirit are what we called the Gifts of Inspiration or of Utterance. They are the vocal Gifts designed as an inspiration in public worship. Of these the Gift of Tongues is by far the most prominent, not to say important. Let us consider it the first of the three.

"Why do you give such prominence to Tongues?" ask our friends of the denominations. Our reply is that we do not. There are three principal reasons why we *seem* to give prominence to this Gift. First, it is the Gift that people are always asking us about and compelling us to discuss. Second, it is the Gift that is manifested in each case when believers receive their Baptism in the Holy Spirit, though other Gifts may be manifested *as well as it:* it is therefore often in evidence. Third, it is among the least of the Gifts, and for that further reason it is by far the most frequently distributed and used. We are compelled to seem to give prominence to this Gift for the same reasons that Paul was compelled to seem to give prominence to it, for he devoted a whole long chapter almost entirely to it, and dismissed the more important Gifts in almost every case in a phrase. The reasons are that the Gift is much misunderstood, and so obviously and arrestingly supernatural that it challenges at once those who do not believe in the supernatural! They are all in doubt, saying one to another, What meaneth this? We are neither always speaking with other tongues nor about them. It is our friends and critics who are always introducing the subject; and of course we delight, like Peter, if they will listen, to answer them according to the

Scripture. It is the easiest thing in the world to reply to critics concerning this Gift, if they really believe the whole of God's Word. The Scripture is so abundantly plain and fulsome on the subject.

What is this Gift of Divers Kinds of Tongues, or Speaking with Tongues? It is supernatural utterance by the Holy Spirit in languages never learned by the speaker—not understood by the mind of the speaker—nearly always not understood by the hearer. It has nothing whatever to do with linguistic ability, nor with the mind or intellect of man. It is a manifestation of the Mind of the Spirit of God employing human speech organs. When a man is speaking with tongues his mind, intellect, understanding are quiescent. It is the faculty of God that is active. Man's will, certainly, is active, and his spirit and his speech organs; but the Mind that is operating is the Mind of God through the Holy Spirit. The linguistic skill of man is no more employed in speaking with tongues than the surgical skill of man was employed when at Peter's word, "Rise and walk," the lame man instantly arose and leaped and walked! It is in short a miracle. It is not a mental miracle; the mentality is God's. It is a vocal miracle.

We must not confuse it with a kind of heaven-aided rhetoric, as when a theology student once said to me, "We had a grand time of liberty in the open air last night: we 'spake with tongues'!" All he meant of course was that they had enjoyed an unusual liberty in English. His words were not strictly truer than if he had said concerning some convert they had had, "we 'raised the dead'."

"But what is the use of speaking with tongues?" we are repeatedly asked, and we are expected to be reduced to impotence and ignominious silence by the query! We rejoicingly take up the challenge, and could easily fill up the remainder of this book with Scripture reasons if we cared to give way to the fault of disproportion.

First let us say that it was the Lord Jesus Himself—your Lord, critical friend! who instituted the Gift of Tongues. He did not limit it to believers in Apostolic days, but promised it to all who would believe. These signs shall follow them that believe; in My Name they shall speak with new tongues (Mark xvi, 17). What would you think of John and Peter if under the shadow of the Cross where Jesus died and where He gave them this promise they had asked, But what is the use of new tongues, Lord Jesus? Is it not just as displeasing to the gracious Lord to hear His people today ask the same unbelieving question? The first important implication here is that all those who have not spoken with new tongues, that neither speak nor seek to speak with new tongues, are outside that group which the Lord Jesus in this verse calls believers; for these signs shall attend them that *believe!* I do not mean that these have not believed on the Lord for salvation: I mean what the Lord means—that they are not among those who are equipped with supernatural powers and sign-gifts that alone in apostate days can attest the authority of the Word they are speaking.

Let us consider some of the Scripture Purposes of Speaking with Tongues.

(a) Speaking with Tongues is the Scriptural evidence of the Baptism in the Holy Spirit.

I say it, and repeat it, with the strongest emphasis in these days when some are letting go the things that have been delivered unto them instead of holding them fast: Speaking with Tongues is the only evidence I see in the Scripture of the Baptism in the Holy Ghost. In Jerusalem at Pentecost when they were filled with the Spirit they "began to speak with other tongues, as the Spirit gave them utterance" (Acts ii, 4). In Caesarea eight years later, on the Gentiles also "was poured out the gift of the Holy Ghost: *for* they heard them speak with tongues" (Acts x, 46). And at Ephesus twenty-three years after Pentecost "the Holy Ghost came on them; and they spake with tongues . . ." (Acts xix, 6). And although at Samaria one year after Pentecost it is not *recorded* that they spake with tongues as they received the Baptism (Acts viii, 17, 19), yet that there *was* a supernatural manifestation is proved by the fact that a Jewish sorcerer already in possession of supernatural power himself (verse 9) should offer money for the greater supernatural power he "saw" (verse 18) and heard before him (cf. Acts ii, 33). Is not the implication irrestible that this miraculous manifestation was the same as at Pentecost, Caesarea and Ephesus: speaking with other tongues? It is not *recorded* that Paul spake with tongues when he received his baptism in the Spirit; but later records make it obvious that he did (Acts ix, 17; 1 Cor. xiv, 18). When anyone in Apostolic days was heard to speak with tongues it was known of a certainty he had received his baptism in the Spirit. Without this sign there was no Scriptural evidence at all. And so today. The first purpose of Tongues is therefore that it provides the Scriptural evidence of the Baptism in the Holy Spirit.

(b) That men may speak supernaturally to God.

Every consecrated believer must have felt at times a consuming desire to open his heart to God in unspeakable communication and adoration inexpressible. There is a deep in the spirit of the redeemed that is never plumbed by the mind or thought. That deep finds expression at last in the Baptism of the Spirit, as unaccustomed words of heavenly coherence sweep up to the Beloved from the newly opened well of the human spirit—flooded as it is with the torrential stream of the divine Spirit. Only deep can call unto deep at the noise of God's full-flowing cataracts. "He that speaketh in a tongue speaketh not unto men but unto God: for no man understandeth him; howbeit in the spirit he speaketh divine secrets" (1 Cor. xiv, 2). The Gift of Tongues sinks a well into the dumb profundities of the rejoicing spirit, liberating a jet of long-pent ecstasy that gladdens the heart of God and man. Blessed fountain of ineffable coherence, of inexpressible eloquence! Have you never in the presence of Jesus felt inarticulate on the very verge of eloquence? This heavenly Gift will loose the spirit's tongue and burst upon the speechless heart with utterance transcending sages' imaginings or angel rhapsodies. Have you never wept to think how helpless your words are to express emotion in the presence of Him whom your soul loveth? Other tongues alone can give you utterance equal to the holy task. Other tongues will give you Names for Jesus that even revelation has not vouchsafed. Other tongues will capture the escaping thought, the elusive expression, the inarticulate longing, lending worthy and soul-satisfying utterance to profoundest gratitude and worship.

An error most persistently cherished by Christians is that on the Day of Pentecost those filled with the Holy Spirit were preaching the gospel to foreigners in foreign languages bestowed for the purpose. The Word quoted above (1 Cor. xiv, 2) makes it clear they were speaking "not unto men but unto God." They were magnifying God for His "wonderful works," now standing out in intensified relief in the new flood of light introduced by the Holy Ghost baptism they had received, and the "foreigners" who were present overheard their rhapsodical praises and marvelled to recognise their own tongues! The notion that the Gift of Tongues was a miraculous bestowal of foreign languages to the early apostles that they might preach the gospel to every creature is an error that could only be held by those who have never taken care to examine all the Scriptures on the subject. Peter was the only one, according to the record, who preached the gospel on the Day of Pentecost, and he employed not other tongues but the universally understood Aramaic, or the equally universal vernacular Greek.

(c) That believers may magnify God (Acts x, 46).

In the house of Cornelius at Caesarea the new converts "spake with tongues and magnified God." What a magnification of the Lord there would be if all Christendom spake with tongues! It is a wonderful word. They *magnified* God. They "made God great" as they broke into the Spirit's rapturous words. There are no terms in natural speech appropriate to the greatness, the excellent greatness of our God. In supernatural speech alone we gain an utterance proportionate to our wondrous Theme and equal to our spirit's strong emotion. With what unimagined eloquence the Spirit's Tongue takes up the Psalmist's heavenly motif, Let such as Love Thy salvation say continually, The Lord be magnified! Make his praise glorious! Those of us who have had the joy of seeing hundreds filled with the Holy Spirit recall that in every case, at the moment of receiving, gesture and upward look and utterance could have no other Object, no other Theme than Jesus; Jesus adorable; Jesus desirable; Jesus most beautiful; Jesus ..! At the extremity of soul ecstasy come other tongues to our relief. The spirit takes up the task: immediately the galleries of our deepest being reverberate with the music of heavenly praise. What could be grander than to tell Jesus all about it in a language that the spirit fully comprehends?

(d) That we may edify ourselves.

He that speaketh in a tongue edifieth himself (1 Cor. xiv, 4). You may edify others by preaching and prophesying and example, but the Scripture indicates this special way of edifying *yourself:* speaking with tongues. Are you edifying yourself? Is it not a good thing to edify yourself? The great apostle thought so, for he edified himself more than all Corinth (1 Cor. xiv, 18)! "Speaking to *yourselves"* (the original significantly has it in Ephesians v, 19; not "to one another" as the R.V.) "in ... spiritual songs," that is songs in other tongues sung to cadences dictated also by the Spirit. Speaking—in songs! Speaking to ourselves thus in the Spirit is edifying ourselves, just as, to use the figure of the previous verse, drinking wine to ourselves is inebriating ourselves. Being filled with the Spirit and yielding to the sweet exercise of speaking or singing with other tongues is building up ourselves, as well as magnifying the Lord and making melody to Him in our hearts (1 Cor. xiv, 15).

If we speak with tongues we have a well within us in this barren wilderness world. Singing thus will start a fountain in the driest desert, "Spring up, O well; Sing ye unto it!" Yes: sing unto the gushing fountain within; so shall its refreshing waters increase. So also in the other figure. The Lord is building us each into something worthy after His plan. By speaking with tongues we help in this upbuilding, edifying, laying course upon course of spiritual substance in the sanctuary for His abiding. Is not that a good purpose?

(e) That our spirits as distinct from our understanding might pray.

"If I pray in a tongue, my spirit prayeth, but my understanding is unfruitful . . . I will pray with the spirit, and I will pray with the understanding also" (1 Cor. xiv, 14). Praying with the spirit is praying in a tongue. The only way to pray with the spirit is to pray in tongues. Do you pray with your spirit, or with your understanding only? How these explicit Holy Ghost teachings are weakened by careless exposition! Praying with the spirit is generally taken to mean praying with the understanding with an access of spiritual power. Praying with the spirit is quite different from praying with the understanding (verse 16). You cannot pray *with* the spirit unless you speak with other tongues. You can pray *in* the Spirit with the *understanding* as in Ephesians vi, 18, but such prayer does not reach the realm of mystery and miracle presided over and directed by the Holy Ghost (1 Cor. xiv, 2). You can neither pray nor sing *with* the spirit (verse 15) unless you speak with tongues. The loose statements of the commentators on these things have the effect, if not the design, of sweeping away the supernatural. Once again it is necessary to warn young Christians against that exegesis that degrades the supernatural in the Bible to the powerless and undistinguished level of the natural. "We know not what we should pray for as we ought." The Spirit both knows and is able. "He maketh intercession for us (and through us) with groanings *that cannot be uttered.*" How often has a Spirit-filled child of God poured forth his soul in agonizing supplication for he knows not what or whom, to find perhaps a year afterwards an echo of his prayer-in-tongues in the miraculous deliverance of some missionary in peril, or some beloved one a thousand miles away at death's door! Think not that these things have no meaning. Praying in tongues is an exercise more potent in its own mysterious realm than the mightiest praying with the understanding. Let us humbly say that those not filled with the Spirit know nothing of these supernatural things. Not for nought has the all-seeing Lord designed an instrument that will reach in its galvanic range circumstances and situations that are infinitely beyond the sweep of poor creature sense and ability.

For "the Searcher of hearts knows what the Spirit's meaning is, because His intercessions for the saints are in harmony with God's will," whereas our human intercessions according to the understanding so often are not (Romans viii, 27, Wey.).

And what a rest to weary mind and nerve, to relax from mental concentration in praying and praising, and break forth in effortless utterance in the Spirit! Notice the blessed connection in Isaiah xxviii, 11, 12: "With stammering lips and another tongue will He speak to this people . . . This is the rest wherewith ye may cause the weary to rest; and this is the refreshing"! What heavenly rest in spiritual exercise has the Lord designed in these heavenly tongues! Hallelujah! "Yet they would not hear" is the Lord's broken cry! How truly fulfilled is this prophecy in the Church of today! Will not *you* hear?

Notice also that through the Gift of Interpretation of Tongues (verse 13) our understanding may know, if the Spirit will, what our spirit prays. Obviously this is not always, nor even often, necessary in private devotions.

(f) That with the Gift of Interpretation of Tongues the Church may be edified.

"Seek that ye may excel to the *edifying* of the church. Wherefore let him that speaketh in a tongue pray that he may interpret. For greater is he that prophesieth than he that speaketh with tongues, except he interpret, that the church may receive *edifying*. Let all things be done unto *edifying*" (1 Cor. xiv, 12, 13, 5, 26).

The three Gifts we are now considering, Tongues, Interpretation and Prophecy, are essentially designed for manifestation in a meeting of believers, and the end of all in their public employment is the edification of the Church. Though the one who speaks with tongues blessedly edifies himself thereby, that edification is confined to himself, his speaking with tongues as such is of no benefit whatever to others. In his private devotions therefore He can edify himself as freely as he will; but in public meetings he must keep silence unless there is one present who possesses the sister Gift of Interpretation of

Tongues. For by speaking with tongues without interpretation a man is speaking only to himself and to God (verse 28). I marvel how those who read this fourteenth chapter, reaching this most beautiful principle of Church edification, can still ask, What is the use of Tongues? Does not their very question suggest that God has made a mistake in adding to the ordinary means of Church edification by the Word and prayer, this extraordinary supernatural way of appeal direct from the Spirit of God to the spirit of man, and then through man's spirit, equally supernaturally, to his mind or "understanding"? If you have not yet felt the need of speaking with tongues may it not be because you have not yet caught the vision of your spirit's helplessness as plainly revealed in the Word, nor yet the vision of God's most entrancing supernatural provision for you and His Church? So overwhelmed am I at the present moment with the heavenly sweetness of this precious endowment that I would with trumpet voice repeat Paul's royal proclamation in the hearing of my brothers and sisters in every Church—"I would that ye all spake with tongues"—that the Church through you might receive edifying. Has the Great Blesser of men really overshot the mark in Tongues and provided something therein that is superfluous or antagonistic to Blessing? Can we really afford to shear off with our petulance or unbelief this mighty detail of His eternal purpose for the Church's blessing just because it does not seem to us in our ignorance a rational shoot from the heavenly stock? Is it really unnatural that a supernatural branch should grow on a supernatural Tree? Would infinite Wisdom take endless pains in a long chapter to prune this precious growth that it might bring forth much fruit in the assemblies if the growth were really a morbid one? Shall we despise or neglect the Gift of Tongues because its miracle-edification is a process not cultivable in human schools nor comprehensible by natural intelligence? Do God's "thoughts" and "ways" stand condemned because they are "higher than the earth?"

(g) Tongues as a sign to them that believe not we will consider in Chapter Fourteen.

(h) Finally Divers kinds of Tongues are among the Gifts divinely appointed for our profit, being manifestations of the Spirit that we may profit withal (1 Cor. xii, 7; Acts ii, 4).

To hear some of our beloved brethren in the opposite camp speak of other tongues one would scarcely imagine that profit was the intention in the Lord's plan or the effect in man's development. As such brethren read these simple comments on God's mighty Word, will they not gratefully accept God's plan for their profit, acknowledge they are in the wrong camp, and come over and help us in the glorious work of building His Church?

These must suffice for our Scripture Purposes.

Let us now take up some thoughts on the Regulation of the Gift.

(1) God says that so far as the public use of the Gift is concerned the proper place to speak with tongues is in a meeting entirely composed of Believers. "If therefore the whole *church* be come together into one place . . ." (verse 23). "How is it then, *brethren?* when *ye* come together, every one of you hath . . . a tongue . . . " (verse 26). "In all churches of the *saints*" (verse 33). To repeat—these Gifts of Inspiration are designed exclusively for the edification of the Church, that is, a company of believers filled with the Holy Ghost and all of them in actual possession of some Gift or "manifestation of the Spirit." There is no mention of them in connection with any gathering such as we today call a Gospel Meeting. We will discuss this when we come to it in the chapter on One Corinthians Fourteen.

(2) Is there a difference between tongues as the initial sign of the Baptism in the Spirit, and the Gift of Tongues for use in the believers' meeting? There is doubt in some minds on this question. Let me give my own well-considered and firm conviction. Everybody speaks in tongues at least once at his Baptism in the Spirit (Acts ii, 4; x, 45, etc.), but apparently all do not retain this power to speak in tongues (1 Cor. xii, 30), though there seems to be no Scripture reason why they should not retain it (1 Cor. xiv, 5, 23). Our experience (my wife's and

mine) in some years at Mr. Howard Carter's Women's Bible School at Louth and Scarborough is that when students have complained that though they spoke with tongues at their Baptism they have since "lost" the power so to speak, in *every* case where there has been expressed desire to renew the blessed exercise the Lord has graciously responded to prayer *at once,* and set the fountain springing again for refreshment at will. The same is true of every Assembly in which we have worked. The only Scriptural distinction between the sign of tongues and the gift of tongues is that when tongues are first employed by an individual, the utterance is the *sign* of the Baptism in the Spirit; every subsequent use of the supernatural tongue by the same individual is the *gift* of tongues in operation. Whether, therefore, the power to speak with tongues after baptism in the Spirit is retained for permanent and public use or not seems to be entirely a matter of personal desire and faith. Some do not wish to go on speaking with tongues. That astonishes me. But the Lord compels nobody anywhere. And the Scripture provides further light on the problem by revealing that there are many who possess Gifts that they never use (1 Tim. iv, 14; 2 Tim. i, 6). The Gift of Tongues is never dead in those who have once spoken in tongues; it may, however, be dormant. A resurgence of the breath of prayer and the blessed sunshine of fervent desire will awake the sleeping Gift, as the springtime revives the vitality of hibernating creatures.

It is the Lord's expressed desire that *all* should speak with tongues (1 Cor. xiv, 5). This makes it clear that though there may be many who do not speak with tongues, it is neither God's design nor fault. "I would ye all spake with tongues" is His clear pronouncement. If you have never thus spoken, seek the Spirit until you do. If you have spoken once but not again, in the Name of the Lord Jesus who filled you with the Holy Spirit, stir up the Gift that *is in you.*

(3) Then the Lord says we can and ought to control the Gift of Tongues.

There is an unfortunate reluctance in some quarters to

accept gracious Scripture safeguards. The Gift is ours when we have received it, and we may use it or misuse it, like any natural gift—conversation, for instance, or fire. It is not the less divine because the occasion and frequency of its use are subject to our own wills. It is not the less authentic because it can be misused. The principle is the same as that which controls Prophecy. "The spirits of the prophets are subject to the prophets" (1 Cor. xiv, 32). Obviously we may speak or not speak in tongues at our own will, since the Lord has placed upon *us* the responsibility for the due restraint as well as the due operation of the Gift. Read 1 Corinthians xiv, 23, and see that though we can all speak at once in other tongues, we must not.

In verse 27 we learn that the number of messages in one meeting is limited to three, "two, or at the most three"; and these not together, but one after another in decent order, that is "by course." The words "two" and "three" refer to different speakers, not to two or three fragments of the one message by the same speaker.

And in verse 28 we are prohibited from speaking with tongues at all if there is no one present with the Gift of Interpretation. Obviously we can and ought to control the Gifts. Any confusion in the use of them arises not from God, but from man's neglect of God's Word. For God is not the Author of confusion, but of peace (verse 33). Man is the Author of any confusion there may be in the employment of the Gifts, and upon him rests responsibility for their regulation. When a man, giving a fourth message in a meeting, says he couldn't help it, and that the Spirit compelled him, he is deceiving himself. God does not break His own Word. Such a man should be lovingly and firmly corrected. The very occasion of these chapters to the Corinthians was the fact that believers were making a disorderly use of a perfectly authentic and blessedly desirable Gift. It is only where there is no life that there is no danger of disorder. If there is life, there must inevitably be disorder to deal with and regulate. The wrong way to deal with disorder is to slay the life; though that is the easiest way, and the way taken by the churches generally. "Where no oxen are, the crib is clean: but much increase is by the strength of the ox"! (Prov. xiv, 4). The nominal church's cribs are clean enough: they have no oxen. There were strong and lovely oxen in the Corinthian crib. The Lord saw some dirt there as a consequence: for the more the oxen, the more the dirt there is to deal with. He sent His servant Paul, not with a poleaxe but with a besom. You can deal with dirt but not with death. Death is the dirtiest dirt. Lord Jesus, give us oxen, and reasonable men like Paul to keep the cribs clean. Much increase is by the strength of the Gifts.

I saw in a room used as a Pentecostal Assembly Hall not long ago a row of fearsome-looking scarlet buckets labelled "FIRE!" Of course they contained *water!* That is the trouble with the churches today. They have got water but no fire. They are much handier with buckets than with brands. Fear is a fine slayer of oxen and quencher of heavenly fire. Yes. Truly. Fire is positively dangerous. Some brands had flown out of the hearth at Corinth on to the nice tidy hearthrug. That was a fault. Paul heard of it and sent along, not a fire extinguisher but a pair of tongs. Don't go without fire in your homes (or Assemblies) because you read of a house (or an Assembly) on fire in the paper yesterday. Fireguards are cheap—and tongs. There is a grand set offered for nothing in One Corinthians Fourteen!—complete with heavenly bellows!

(4) Then God expressly says we must not forbid to speak with tongues (verse 39).

This does not mean, of course, that we must not forbid disorderly speaking with tongues, but that we must not forbid speaking with tongues entirely. What have the leaders of the other churches and chapels to say to this command of God? To say that the Gifts of the Spirit were limited to Corinth or the early apostolic Church is to admit the vicious principle of Bible criticism and selection that has been responsible for the blasphemies of Modernism. There is just as much Scripture authority for saying that the Cross was limited to Corinth and the early Church as that tongues were. And how can those "ministers" who claim they possess today the Spiritual Gifts of "Wisdom" and "Knowledge" (abasing them to the level of natural gifts of learning and speech)—how can they consistently pretend that the remaining Gifts are not with us now! FORBID NOT TO SPEAK WITH TONGUES! I would write the words on every spire and tower and gable and "altar" and pulpit in Christendom. Why not? Are they not as truly the Words of the Lord as, If ye love Me, keep My commandments?

(5) Edification is always the test of the Gift's proper employment—Let all things be done unto edifying (verse 26), and decency and order are its only safeguard (verse 40). Since the temptation to display is very strong in these vocal Gifts, especially this marvellously arresting Gift of Tongues, so generously distributed by the Spirit, we ought to be more anxious to guard and regulate it according to God's very exact instructions.

With a few brief observations we must leave this enthralling Gift for another chapter. "Do you understand what you say when you speak with tongues?" "No" "Does anybody else understand what you say?" "No." "Then what is the use of tongues?" We smile to recall how often we have recorded our unashamed negatives in the above questionnaire! To the more than sufficient explanations included in this chapter I will add that God Himself ordained that tongues should be "unknown," otherwise there would be no reason in His having further instituted the Gift of Interpretation of Tongues to make them "known."

An objection is sometimes raised that tongues, though necessary on the Day of Pentecost because foreigners were present, are not necessary now, for foreigners are not present in our meetiings. I have already said— at (b) above—that the gospel was not preached to these foreigners in their own tongues by the 120, but by Peter only in a natural tongue. Further there was no diversity of nationalities present at Caesarea (Acts x, 46), nor at Ephesus (Acts xix, 6), not at Corinth (1 Cor. xiv, 23), yet they spoke with tongues at all three places.

Then there is a notion abroad that tongues are a kind of gibberish, incoherent and non-intelligible, a series of uninterpretable glossal noises. No. Tongues were and are languages. They are mostly unknown to the hearers and always to the speakers. But they might on occasion be known to the hearers, as at Pentecost, where the tongues were unknown as they were spoken and known as they were heard. That not only constituted but proved the miracle. And the same thing often occurs today. Our missionaries are always giving us instances. A Chinese student named Wang, aged seventeen, received the Baptism in the Spirit at Luh Hsi, China, in 1927. Speaking in other tongues he was clearly understood in English, a language not a word of which he knew. His very words are recorded by the missionary who heard him. "Those that walk with Him in white and are faithful will ascend at His appearing. Behold, He is coming very soon!" Wang knew nothing of the coming of the Lord. Mr. Burton of the Congo was present in Preston as a brother received his Baptism and spoke with tongues. The language he spoke was Kiluba, as familiar to Mr. Burton as English. One of our missionaries, also of the Congo, was present when a young man of his black flock received the Baptism in the Holy Ghost. He was amazed to hear the man speaking in perfect English, repeating Old Testament instances of creation and history. He knew no word of English and nothing of the instances he was recording. The missionary was so astonished at this mighty miracle that he left the hut in search of his wife as witness. When he returned with his wife the man was still speaking in his English "unknown tongue," but he had changed over to New Testament revelation concerning the imminent coming again of the Lord. Instances could be multiplied.

Some people despise tongues, because they are often spoken by those who obviously have no learning of any sort. Did not some people despise Jesus for similar reasons? The mightiest Apostle did not despise tongues. On the contrary he spake with tongues more than they all, and thanked God for the privilege (1 Cor. xiv, 18).

Speaking with tongues is not for guidance or direction in personal matters, but for edification, exhortation and comfort, like the Gift of Prophecy—to which with Interpretation it is compared as an equivalent (1 Cor. xiv, 3-5). This is most seriously important. Seeking guidance by Tongues and Interpretation in little groups in private rooms is not only unscriptural but highly mischievous. In others' hearing the Gift is for use in the Assembly only. If we use the Gift in private at home we must "speak to ourselves and God" alone (v. 28). The word of God, and sometimes certain other greater Gifts, are for guidance. And these never at the will of man but only as God wills to reveal. Never Tongues and Interpretation alone.

We must expect religious people to express bewilderment and disapproval and to mock us when we speak with tongues. "They were all amazed." What meaneth this?" "These men are full of new wine!" (Acts ii, 5, 12-14). But like Peter we can confidently rise and give them, if they will listen, Scriptural authority and vindication.

Speaking with Tongues is a glorious exercise and a blessed Gift of our gracious Lord, but it is not the most important thing. It is the least of the Gifts, and for that reason the commonest.

But finally we will not forget that Peter claimed that speaking with tongues was the direct fulfilment of Joel's prophecy of the outpouring of the Spirit (Joel ii, 28, 29). "What meaneth this?" they asked in amazement. Not, What meaneth this concourse of people—this unaccustomed excitement—this carnival of joy—this talk of "rushing wind" and "flames"—this looking intently up to heaven? Not even, What meaneth this strange outpouring of the Spirit? No. What they were fearfully and wonderingly asking was, How came these peasant folk to be speaking cultured languages they obviously never learned? What meaneth this SPEAKING WITH MIRACULOUS TONGUES? This speaking with tongues, said Peter in reply, is that which was spoken by the prophet Joel!,... "In the last days, saith God, I will pour out My Spirit ... "!

Have you received for yourself the fulfilment of Joel's glorious prophecy?

CHAPTER TWELVE

Interpretation of Tongues

. . . to another the interpretation of tongues. 1 Cor. xii, 10.

It will have been obvious to all that of the Nine Gifts of the
Spirit, seven are common to both Testaments while the
remaining two have come into operation only since Pentecost.
These two are the most closely related of all the Gifts. They
are Tongues and Interpretation.

But when we say they are closely related we must not
suppose that they are so dependent one upon the other that
one is useless without the other. Certainly Interpretation of
Tongues could have no meaning whatever without the Gift of
Tongues. In this it is unique among the Gifts. But Other
Tongues is not in the same absolute sense dependent upon
Interpretation, for it has its own delightful purpose as we have
seen in the edification of the individual spirit quite apart from
its further purpose by the sisterly aid of this precious Gift of
Interpretation.

Interpretation of Tongues is the supernatural showing forth
by the Spirit of the meaning of an utterance in other tongues.
This interpretation is not an operation of the mind of the
interpreter but the mind of the Spirit of God. The interpreter
never understands the tongue he is interpreting, and it is no
part of his task to provide equivalent terms in his own tongue
for the supernatural words spoken. They are unknown words:
so much so that they are quite indistinguishable in the phrases
of which they form part. The interpretation is just as much a
miracle as the original utterance in tongues. Both are utterances equally direct from the mind of the Spirit of God.

Indeed a believer possessing this Gift of Interpretation of

Tongues pays no heed whatever to the terms spoken in the unknown language he is to interpret; he just looks to God as dependently for the showing forth of the meaning as the speaker in tongues looked in full dependence and ignorance to God for his supernatural utterance. In the mind of God, of course, the two operations are exactly and most blessedly linked; in the mind of men the two utterances are quite independent and equally direct from God. That constitutes the mighty miracle both of Tongues and Interpretation.

Right down the list of the Gifts misconception and misrepresentation have been at work ignoring or denying or destroying their supernatural character and power; and even this beautiful Gift has not escaped the adversary's attention. It is almost inconceivable that there should be those who abbreviate the title of the Gift, calling it the Gift of Interpretation, looking upon it as merely an acute sense of spiritual values, or an unusually apt unfolding of the Word of God. Yet there are such. We must with all our powers guard the Gifts from every attempt to reduce them to the natural plane. This Gift is not a general power of clear explanation in spiritual matters: it is a precise Gift if entirely miraculous Interpretation of TONGUES.

The purposes of the Gift are easily and soon stated.

It is first of all to render the Gift of Tongues intelligible to others, so that the Church, as well as the possessor of the Gift, may be edified thereby. "Let one interpret" ... "that the church may receive edifying" (1 Cor. xiv, 27, 5). Even a cursory reading of this fourteenth chapter will show that this Gift, with the two others. Tongues and Prophecy, is exclusively for use in assembly of believers.

Another use of the Gift, quite subsidiary to the one above, is that it can make clear to the understanding of the possessor what has already been an edification of his spirit in other tongues (verses 13,14). It is obviously not necessary that everything we utter in private in other tongues should be clear to our understanding; but in circumstances where an interpretation is necessary or desirable, God will give one, that the understanding may profit as well as the spirit. But let us not make the mistake of supposing that no good is done because our understanding is inactive: for the spirit is profiting richly as we speak in tongues in private, even while the understanding remains quite "unfruitful." So far as assembly meetings are concerned we are to excel to the edifying not of ourselves but of the church, and the Gift of Interpretation has this end principally, if not exclusively, in view. Read carefully once more the verses 12 and 13. And notice that in verses 14 to 17 those present can say Amen to your prayer or your message in a natural tongue they understand, and also to your prayer or message in supernatural tongues when it is made clear to the understanding by this Gift; but that without this Gift the most obviously authentic and fervent speaking with tongues is unprofitable in the assembly; such uninterpreted speaking is therefore expressly prohibited (28).

A few observations on the Regulation of the Gift, and a few considerations of some oft-repeated questions, will complete our brief study.

(a) Once again most of the obstacles to our clear understanding of the Gift vanish when we consider the exact title of the Gift. It is the Gift of Interpretation—not Translation—of Tongues. A translation is a rendering from one language to another in equivalent words or grammatical terms. An interpretation is a declaration of the meaning (see v. 11), and may be very differently stated from the precise form of the original. It may be pictorial, parabolic, descriptive or literal, according to the urge of the Spirit or the character of the one interpreting. The Greek word in the original means "to explain thoroughly"—not to translate. It is more of a transposition than a translation—as when Joseph showed forth the meaning of the baker's and the butler's dreams. Jesus gave an interpretation of the parable of the tares when he transposed the terms from the natural to the spiritual (Matt. xiii, 24-30 and 36-43). And in Matt. vi, 26-34, the words that Jesus spoke, presumably in Aramaic, are of course appropriately *translated* in our authorized version as: "Behold the fowls of the air . . . Consider the lilies of

149

the field . . . " and following; another suitable *translation* is given by Weymouth as "Look at the birds which fly in the air . . . Learn a lesson from the wild lilies . . . "; but a perfectly legitimate if prosaic *interpretation* might have been: "The heavenly Father is a universal Provider for those who look up to Him. He will find you clothing and renew it as He gives new feathers to the moulted birds. He will even take care moreover that the garments are beautiful, if need be, as is His custom with the wild flowers. He will give you food when you are hungry, just as He finds berries and insects for the wild birds. You need therefore never have any undue anxieties about daily provision."

Many varieties of expression might be employed and many details added without materially altering the sense of the words so far as the simple message is concerned. Of course I do not mean that my awkward paraphrase would be equally inspired with the exact Scripture words. I am just using an illustration to show how an interpretation differs from a translation, or transliteration, and how much more liberty of expression there is in an interpretation than in a translation.

This at once explains the (to some people) mystifying circumstance that sometimes the utterance in tongues is much briefer than the subsequent showing forth in interpretation, or the reverse. The interpreter is not translating. The Holy Spirit is explaining the meaning in a miracle utterance.

The interpretation can be, however, a literal translation of the message in tongues; for of course the Spirit is at liberty to dictate what words He will. Many an instance might be cited of an utterance in tongues receiving an exact literal translation in the hearing of one familiar with the language spoken, and therefore in a position to verify it.

Why should it be thought a thing incredible that God, the Author (and Confuser) of Tongues, can both speak His own Tongues and impose them, learned or unlearned, upon the speech organs of whom He will? Is not the whole meaning of the supernatural in the Bible, and in this Holy Ghost movement today, that being contrary to the natural, and therefore dark to the human senses, it produces what the Lord Jesus calls the "impossible"? And is not the effect of this supernatural to show us a God infinitely lifted up above us, and infinitely able to do beyond our natural imaginings? And why should a God who spake with His own Naked Voice in Hebrew from the fiery top of Sinai; who spake by a cherub in Chaldean to the presumptuous Babylonish monarch "flourishing" in his palace; who commanded His "anointed shepherd" Cyrus concerning His beloved Israel in Persian—why can He not in tongue of any tribe or people or nation, living or dead, either by His own awful Voice or through the lips of whomsoever He will, supernaturally communicate with His people today? And why, having supernaturally conveyed to His people of old the heavenly land flowing with milk and honey; having distributed to them by a thousand miracles the hills and vales and pastures and brooks and grapes and pomegranates of that land—why should He not bestow upon His spiritual Israel today, equally supernaturally, the very languages of that land—Hittitish and Jebusitish and Amoritish and Horonitish; or equally miraculously the living languages of today, and withal equally supernaturally the various interpretations thereof? Since God can think in Chinese, speak in Polish and hear you thinking— assenting or protesting—in English, all at the same time; and since He can make an ass speak Hebrew (I say it in all seriousness)—can He not make me His mouthpiece in whatsoever language He pleases, and you His interpreter in whatsoever other tongue He will, if you yield to His plan?

(b) The temperament, natural gifts and training, as well of course, as the nationality, of the possessor of the Gift will influence the statement, but the Gift is not for that reason the less supernatural. Two youths, for instance, might be sent by their employer with the same message to the same person. One might say, My governor cannot let you have the things you ordered. The other, sent as a safety measure in case the first somehow miscarried, might say, Mr. Smith regrets that owing to a careless oversight in the hardware department he finds himself unable to supply the goods he promised. Both messengers convey the principle message; the difference in disposition, training and experience accounts for the difference in expression. The Lord equally entrusts His revelations to sanctified farm-hands and God-fearing, anointed philosophers. The farm-hand will deliver his message with the blunt forthrightness of an Amos; the philosopher with the refinement of an Isaiah. But remember that much correspondence with the sweet heavenly sanctities will transform the crudities of a Galilean bumkin into the miraculous and exalted subtleties of the epistles of John.

(c) Those who speak in other tongues are expressly instructed to pray for this further Gift (v. 13).

It is significant that though Interpretation is not exclusively distributed among those who already speak with tongues, yet these are by far the commonest possessors of the Gift. So far as my own experience is concerned it is very rarely that we find one who interprets who does not with equal freedom speak with tongues.

The first thing to notice here is that God does not wish to silence those who speak with tongues. On the contrary He wishes them to enjoy greater freedom in the exercise of their precious Gift. Therefore He does not instruct that those who speak with tongues should limit their supernatural exercise to their private devotions; but that they might equally profit by the public use of the Gift, and at the same time give others the advantage of profiting thereby, He instructs them to seek the added supernatural power to interpret (verse 13). There will be only a few who are "zealous" enough to seek thus; these are those who greatly rejoice in the indescribable blessing of speaking with tongues (verse 12). Then perhaps this verse 13, considered with 14 and 15, is an indication more definite than my tentative remarks in the last chapter under (e) suggested, that the Lord will grant private interpretations where desirable. Further, this same verse 13 confirms the suggestion of 1 Corinthians xii, 30, that there are many who do not speak with tongues, because they neglect God's special invitation in xiv, 5. And lastly this verse shows how generously Interpretation is distributed by the Spirit, since all who speak with tongues are encouraged to seek and receive it. Which quite naturally leads us to our next thought:

(d) "Let one interpret" (27)

What is the meaning of this verse? Many views are held, and therefore many practices are represented in our assemblies. But the words must have a clear, definite meaning, if we can find it.

Personally I am fully convinced it does not mean that the same individual must always interpret in all meetings, nor even that the same person must interpret all messages in the one meeting. After the Gift of Tongues this Gift of Interpretation is by far the most generously distributed of the Gifts. What would be the purpose of such a general bestowal of powers that, for all that, are to be limited to odd individuals here and there? There are a score or more who can interpret even in a smallish assembly. They never get a chance of using their precious Gift. The Lord, I feel certain, wishes every one of these in turn to taste the sweetness of the words of the Spirit on his redeemed lips through this Gift.

"Let one interpret" first of all means that where there is speaking with tongues (as instructed in this verse), somebody *must* interpret. If you read the verse again you will see that is really all that it says. Take the Twentieth Century translation: "If any of you use the gift of 'tongues,' not more than two, or at the most three, should do so—each speaking in his turn—and some one should interpret them. If there is no one able to interpret what is said, they should remain silent at the meeting of the Church . . . " The word "one" is not a numeral, like the words "two" and "three" in the same verse; it is a pronoun, meaning somebody—of course in the singular, "Also, let someone interpret" (Moffatt).

But if we put the verse together with verse 30 we shall learn another lesson from it—a lesson that is conveyed by the spirit of the whole chapter. Verse 30 forbids selfishness and strife in the use of the Gifts. One individual message must receive not more than one interpretation, even though a dozen worshippers might have been able to interpret it. Some one—not some two or three—must interpret each message.

The purpose of this regulation is therefore no doubt twofold: first, that there shall be no refusal to interpret where tongues are legitimately employed; and second, that there shall be no competition among interpreters in the showing forth of the Spirit's meanings (see verse 11): for true it is that some have gifts of interpretation far in advance of others: such might feel, as they hear one interpret, that they could give a more adequate unfolding of the message in tongues—and no doubt in many cases they could; they are, however, to "hold their peace" (30); the Lord prohibits competitive utterances, and graciously grants equal unction and authority to messages that, like eagles, soar in heavenly eloquence, or, like wildwood flowers, almost forget themselves in beautiful reserve.

The Lord intends that His saints shall enjoy the same liberty in interpreting as in speaking with tongues: that as many as three shall contribute to the meeting's blessing with their Gift of Tongues, and that different speakers, not more than three, should minister their Gift of Interpretation. What can "every one of you . . . hath an interpretation" in verse 26 mean if God really wished to say "*only* one of you" hath an interpretation, while *every* one of you hath a psalm or a doctrine or a tongue or a revelation? If the interpretations are limited to the same speaker in every meeting why are not the tongues and psalms and doctrines also so limited?

At the same time I feel very strongly that in great meetings or even small assemblies, where there is a likelihood of some fanatical or selfish person misusing the Gift, the leader of the meeting or the assembly should take all the interpretations until he is sure of his ground. If he does not possess the Gift, all he has to do is to obey verse 13 and believe God.

I am conscious that in saying these (and many other) things I am going somewhat contrary to the established custom in many very blessed assemblies; but I trust it is with humility and grace I am promoting such thoughts as I am convinced cannot but be in harmony with the Word of God.

(e) Recently there has arisen a controversy round the word "message" as applied to public utterances in tongues. Why? Surely those words that are intended as supernatural communications from the Holy Spirit to believers through the Gifts of Tongues and Interpretation can be appropriately and profitably referred to as messages!

I have heard it objected that because in tongues men are speaking to God and not to men the interpretations that purport to speak messages to *men* are therefore not properly in order. But were not the 120 speaking to God at Pentecost? And did not what was overheard come as messages to the devout Jews? Was not the recital to God of His "marvellous works" a recital to men of the same works? And was it not exactly this that constituted the message and convicted the hearers of their need of that same knowledge of God? When, for instance, the Psalmist says to God, Thou desirest truth in the inward parts, is it not at once a message to us that God requires truth in the inward parts? And can we not therefore at once transpose it from the second person into the third and say with all Scripture authority, God requires men to be truthful, not only with their lips, but also in their hearts? And is not that really a very good and honest interpretation of what David says, and what God means him to say to us? Suppose that in other tongues one were saying to God, O Lord, Thou lovest the humble and resistest the proud, would it not be a perfectly good and truthful interpretation on the lips of another: THE Lord loveth the humble and resisteth the proud? Is not much of Scripture truth conveyed to us in this very way, as we overhear men of God talking to God Himself concerning His qualities and requirements? . . . "There is no God like Thee, in heaven above, or on earth beneath, who keepest covenant and mercy with Thy servants that walk before Thee with all their hearts." Is not that a message to you?

And if some "messages" in tongues (as friends further object) turn out to be praises or prayers, can they not by the Spirit find appropriate expression in interpretation   the praise in tongues coming out as praise in interpretation, and the prayers coming out as prayer? And would it constitute a calamity of major importance if in course of interpretation the prayer or praises even got transposed into exhortations or comforts? Is there really much difference in blessing to our hearts between, "Lord, help us!" or "We bless Thee that Thou helpest us!" or "The Lord will help us!"—one prayer, one praise and the other exhortation?

It is clear also that both "blessing" and "thanksgiving" may be the character of the message in tongues, and therefore of that follows them (16, 17).

(f) Giving a message in other tongues and interpreting oneself would seem to be not unscriptural (5), and many of us have richly enjoyed the ministry of beloved brethren in this way; but the weight of Scripture is all on the side not of monopoly but sharing in the contribution of spiritual ministry through the Gifts. Read verses 12 and 26. Verse 5 is really not indicating the purpose of the Gift of Interpretation, but rather dropping it into the scale with Tongues to show their combined value as compared with Prophecy.

(g) From verse 27 and what has been said under (d) above it will be clear that when in any meeting three messages in tongues have been interpreted, no interpreter, however much he may feel the weight of unction or the urge of the Spirit, must interpret a fourth. No mightiest pressure of unction can ever be taken as an encouragement to us to break the Word of God. Let a man use his blessed overplus of unction in prayer or praise or faith or Amens, or perhaps in some of those other ministries suggested in verse 26— which we will further consider when we reach it in Chapter Fourteen.

(h) And lastly, even when we possess the Gift of Interpretation we shall need more faith for its operation than for an utterance in tongues. One reason for this is that since what we say in interpretation is understood by our minds our adversary has more likelihood of silencing us by the inevitable suggestion that we are "making it up." Has the enemy never made the same vile suggestion to you concerning the glories of heaven and your lovely salvation? It is moreover a principle that the greater the Gift the greater the faith needed for its operation. For this reason many a reader will have no need to ask God for the Gift of Interpretation: he will rather have to listen to the voice of the Word still commanding—Stir up the gift that is *in* thee!—that the Church may receive edifying, and that the Lord Jesus may be abundantly magnified through His own appointed heavenly and supernatural agencies.

CHAPTER THIRTEEN

Prophecy

. . .to another prophecy. 1 Cor. xii, 10.

PROPHECY! What human words shall reach the splendours of
so high a theme? What hands can more than mar its pure
brightness? By the spurting of its own fountain in the spirit
can its beauty be felt, even tasted; but how can we with sin-
blunted sense unearth for fellow mortals the mysteries of so
rare a fount?

To *"flow forth"* is the lovely meaning of the commonest
Hebrew word. Naba! To "bubble forth, like a fountain" says
one. As the heart of the Psalmist when it was bubbling up or
boiling over with a good matter touching the King! Hallelujah!
"To let drop" is the meaning of another delightful Hebrew word:
to let drop like golden oil in ripened olive yards; or honey from
the crammed honeycomb; or sparkling rain from the bursting
clouds. And the meaning of yet another Hebrew word is *"to
lift up"* – like coloured banners with mystic devices, or silver
clarions with flourishes of solemnity or delight. To flow
forth–tumble forth–spring forth! You that prophesy!–do not
these Hebrew words exactly describe your precious fountain?
Who would not covet thus to prophesy (xiv, 39)?

To "speak for another" is the meaning of the Greek word.
To speak for God! To be His "spokesman," His "mouth"!
Wherefore, brethren, covet to prophesy. By the Gift of
Prophecy the Holy Ghost makes you, O once injurious,
unprofitable, the "mouth" of the Lord! Therefore (you can
say) my heart is glad, and my glory rejoiceth. And my mouth
shall praise thee with joyful lips!

But lest we linger too long on the exalted heights, like Dan

158

whom the Amorites would not suffer to come down to the valley, we will descend at once to the lowly plains and learn, in the only way that earth-dwellers can, by diligent and prayerful toiling at the Word.

Prophecy, though last in order as we for convenience have taken it, is really the most important of the three Gifts of Inspiration or Utterance. The importance of the Gift can be gauged from the fact that some form of the word occurs twenty-two times in these chapters in Corinthians, eleven to fourteen. The unusual frequency of the word indicates not only the importance of the Gift but the urgency of the need for its regulation. The sharper the tool the more need for care in its employment.

Prophecy in its simplest form is divinely inspired and anointed utterance. It is entirely supernatural. As speaking with tongues is supernatural utterance in an unknown tongue, so Prophecy is supernatural utterance in a known tongue. It is a manifestation of the Spirit of God, and not of the human mind (xii, 7). It has no more to do with human powers of thought and reasoning than walking on water has to do with human powers of equilibrium. It is a miracle. It is an act straight from heaven, just as giving sight to blind eyes by a touch of human hands is an act from heaven. In its simplest form it may be possessed by all who have received the Baptism in the Holy Ghost; "for ye may all prophesy one by one" (xiv, 31). The human will and faith are active in prophecy—but not the human intellect. Its pronouncements, therefore, come with the same divine authority and power from the lips of a peasant or a philosopher, for both are but "mouths" for the expression of divine words.

Such a lovely Gift we may be sure will provide much occasion for the cunning manipulations of the enemy. Since he cannot dam so rich a stream, that has begun to flow again from under the holy threshold this wonderful quarter of a century, he will divert it or vitiate it or slander it or exalt it, or in some other way reduce its authority or attractiveness or usefulness or appeal. We must therefore, with patience and affection towards those who have fallen into some degree of error in this beautiful spiritual exercise, look first at some of the mistaken views of the Gift.

(a) Most important of all—the Gift of Prophecy is confused with the Prophetic Office.

To fail to distinguish between the Gift and the Office is to abuse the one and degrade the other. This very failure has quite dimmed the pure glory of a whole branch of this blessed Holy Ghost movement. It is not really difficult to convince our dear brethren of their error if they will only listen as we consider together the Scriptures they love. Surely no views are so fixed in any of us that they cannot bear afresh the blazing flood-light of God's pure Word!

Admittedly everything is radically changed in the New Testament order. There is hardly more relationship between the Old Testament and the New Testament "prophet" than there is between the Old Testament and the New Testament "priest." Both have become much less critical because much more common or numerous. In the Old Testament only some were priests, because such intermediaries were necessary; in the New Testament all are priests. because our Antitypical Priest has come and is Himself seated in heaven as our only Intermediary. In the same way in the Old Testament, only some were prophets, because such intermediaries were necessary; but in the New Testament "all may prophesy" since our Antitypical Prophet has taken up the Office and sent forth a Representative who will lead us all equally into all truth. True the Office of Prophet still exists, but there is obviously a difference, not only between this and the Old Testament Office, but also between this and the New Testament Gift of Prophecy. All may now seek to prophesy (xiv, 1): this was not so in the Old Testament. And again all may seek to prophesy, though not all are called upon to be Prophets (xii, 28, 29). To understand this difference we must narrowly scan not only the word "prophet", but also the word "gift."

Both the offices and the spiritual endowments are called "gifts" (Eph, iv, 8, 11; 1 Cor. xii, 28, 30); but the Offices are the gifts of Jesus to the *Church*, while the Gifts in 1 Corinthains xii and xiv are the *gifts* of the Holy Spirit to the individual. And again, both holders of the Prophetic Office and holders of the Gift of Prophecy are called "prophets"; yet there is a difference—a difference which is clearly seen in Acts xxi, 9, 10, where Philip's four daughters, "which did prophesy" are put in deliberate contradistinction to "a certain PROPHET named Agabus" who in inspired mimic action *foretold* how Paul should go to Jerusalem and what should befall, him there. Those "who prophesy" are *prophets* certainly, but they are not PROPHETS in the grand sense, either of the Old Testament or the New.

Let us for clearness set out our reasons in categorical order. The Prophetic Office and the Gift of Prophecy are distinct for the following reasons:

1. The Office, of Prophet is inseparable from a *person* (Eph. iv. 11); the Gift of Prophecy is only an instrument (1 Cor. xii, 10). This instrument, the Prophetic Gift of the Spirit, does not qualify for the Prophetic Office. Far greater gifts than the simple gift of prophecy are needed to make a man a PROPHET. The exhortation in Cor. xiv, 1, is not to seek an office but a Gift of the Spirit. Seeking after offices is the cause of many evils. The Scripture forbids it. Desiring Spiritual Gifts is a good thing. Scripture encourages it.

But our "Apostolic" friends make a difference between "prophets" and "set prophets" in the New Testament. The Scripture hints no such difference. "Set prophets" are an anomaly adopted in error to fit a human system of church government. They can be finally dismissed in a sentence. There is not a shred more *Scripture* authority for "set" prophets than there is for "set" speakers in other tongues (1 Cor. xii, 28).

2. Revelation of things outside the Word of God—things of the hidden past, present or future—is necessary to the Prophetic Office, as David, who "being a *prophet* and *knowing* that God had sworn with an oath to him, that of the fruit of his loins, according to the flesh, he would raise

up Christ to sit on his throne; he, *seeing this before,* spake of the resurrection of Christ . . ." (Acts 11, 30). But this revelation is not included in the scope of the Spiritual Gift of Prophecy given in Corinthians xiv, 3. The test of the PROPHET is this personal and exclusive revelation (Num. xii, 6); but I Corinthians xiv does not anywhere imply any such personal revelation to those prophesying. The third verse plainly limits the province of the Gift of the Spirit to edification, exhortation, and comfort.

If from this point for a page or two, when we are speaking of the Office of Prophecy or the holder of it, we adopt bold letters, thus **(prophecy, prophet)**; and when we refer to the simple New Testament Gift of Prophecy or its owner, we use capital letters, thus (PROPHECY, PROPHET) the distinctions will be clearer.

3. The Gift of Prophecy is compared with the Gift of Tongues plus Interpretation (xiv, 5) in such a way as to suggest an exact correspondence in value. Nobody would say that the two Gifts of Tongues and Interpretation place their possessor among the Seers! Neither does the equivalent Gift of PROPHECY.

4. The Gift of PROPHECY comes well down the list in order of importance among the Gifts (1 Cor. xii, 10): the **Prophetic Office** is second among the offices (Eph. iv, 11; I Cor. xii, 28). If the Prophetic Gift qualified for the Prophetic Office we should expect a more exact correspondence in their enumeration. Naturally the greater Office includes the lesser Gift—but not the reverse.

5. Among the holders of the **Prophetic Office** are such mighty names as Moses, Elijah, David, Isaiah, Paul! We shall see that the addition of further and mightier Gifts is necessary to place a person among the Seers. Any ordinary believer—everybody—(xiv, 31) may be the possessor of the Gift of PROPHECY, but obviously not of the Office. If the contrary were true we should be inudated with prophets to the exclusion of pastors, teachers, evangelists, and so on. Clearly each of these latter may be PROPHETS—but not

prophets. You remember that at Ephesus as Paul laid hands on the new believers that they might receive the Holy Ghost, each of them spake with tongues, and all of them PROPH-ESIED! (Acts xix, 6.) That surely does not mean that each of those raw recruits became a **prophet** in the grand sense, like David! If all may PROPHESY, and every PROPHET thus became a **prophet** where would be the room for the ministry of **prophets**?

For these and other reasons the Prophetic Office is distinct from the Gift of Prophecy.

(b) A further mistake is that the Gift is confused with Prediction.

This, too, is extremely important. Careful examination will show that the Gift does not in itself convey the power to predict the future. The Scripture definition in 1 Corinthians xiv, 3, gives no hint of foretelling.

As I have said above, the word "prophet" simply means "one who speaks for another." It was only in medieval times that the word passed into the English language in the sense of *prediction* which is its popular meaning today. "Etymologic-ally," says William Smith in his Bible Dictionary, "it is certain that neither prescience nor prediction is implied by the term in the Hebrew, Greek, or English language."

To PROPHESY, then, does not mean to foretell, but simply to speak for another. PROPHECY may certainly be employed as the medium of prediction, as a river may bear upon its bosom a floating flower, or a wisp of moss or a branch or a boat; but PROPHECY in itself is a simple stream flowing independently and gracefully through happy Pentecost meadows. If it uncovers or foretells, it is carrying something else not native to it. It is like a lovely horse—sometimes alone or just bestridden by its equerry; sometimes carrying a singing youth, sometimes a herald, or a guardsman or a hunter or a discoverer. Thus sometimes the simple PROPHET is bestridden by the greater, much more important **prophet**. Or to drop the metaphors, if in PROPHESYING a revelation is given of some

163

existing fact quite hidden from the senses, the Word of Knowledge is operating with the simple Gift of PROPHECY. If an event is predicted (an event, of course, that really comes to pass, like the death foretold by Agabus in Acts xi, 28), then the Word of Wisdom is working in conjunction with PROPHECY. In 1 Corinthians xiv, 6, we see this possibility of several gifts operating in association at the same time. A beautiful example of the use of the simple Gift of PROPHECY is seen in Luke i, 46-55: "And Mary said, My soul doth magnify the Lord, and my spirit hath rejoiced in God my Saviour . . . ." Only once in this lovely passage are the reins taken by the greater **Prophecy**, when at verse 48, in a Word of Wisdom, Mary predicts: "For, behold, from henceforth all generations shall call me blessed." When the simple Gift is regularly accompanied with the exercise of these greater Gifts its possessor may be regarded as a **prophet** or a **seer**.

Revelation of the future is *always* the work of the Word of Wisdom, and never of the simple Gift of PROPHECY. The revelations of the Epistles (and indeed of the whole of Scripture) are one sustained flow of PROPHETIC utterance, lavishly laden with future revelations of the Word of Wisdom. Concerning these revelations of the Epistle writers, revelation naturally came more often through PROPHECY then than it does now, because then there was no New Testament available for guidance.

Future revelation may come also through visions and dreams and mimetic gesture, etc., as Daniel's and Ezekiel's and John's (Num. xii, 6). The *word* that conveys miraculous revelation is PROPHECY—and the word only; the *work* of revelation is the work of some other and greater gift. When Ezekiel "prophesied" life to the bones and they lived the power was in the associated Gift of Faith—not in the prophetic word. The same with the Lord when He prophesied death to the fig tree and it perished. And the word of the Lord that told the disciples where to find the colt tied was a simple word of PROPHECY: the revelation it contained came to the Lord by a Word of Knowledge. And so on with many of the Gifts.

Sometimes the simple stream of PROPHECY is laden with a burden of prophetic prayer, as in the fifth Psalm: "Give ear to my word, O Lord! consider my meditation Hearken unto the voice of my cry, my King and my God: for unto thee I will pray." The whole Psalm, by the very feel of it in our spirits, is prayer in the Holy Ghost, as in Ephesians vi, 18 and Jude 20, with an anointing and an exalted utterance soaring into heavenly PROPHECY, most moving and soul-stirring.

Sometimes the burden is one of praiseful worship, as in Psalm viii: "O Lord, our Lord, how excellent is Thy Name in all the earth! who hast set thy glory above the heavens!..." (cf. 1 Chron. xxv, 3, 5). And sometimes the voice of PROPHECY swells into a paean of rapturous gratitude, wonder, adoration—magnifying the Lord for His blessed Deliverances: "The Lord is my strength and song, and He is become my salvation: He is my God, and I will prepare Him an habitation; my father's God and I will exalt Him ... Who is like unto Thee, O Lord, among the mighty ones? Who is like Thee, glorious in holiness, fearful in praises, doing wonders?"

(c) Arising out of the former error (b) and closely related to it is the mistaken notion that PROPHECY is intended for guidance. Let us consider this separately.

Guidance is not indicated as one of its uses in the comprehensive definition in 1 Corinthians xiv, 3. It is not—indeed no spiritual gift is—intended to take the place of common sense and natural judgment. "Be not as the horse, or as the mule, which have no understanding," says the Psalmist. "Yea, and why even of yourselves judge ye not what is right?" says the Lord Jesus (Psalm xxxii, 9; Luke xii, 57). Here again our "Apostolic" friends go badly off the Scripture lines in giving "Readings" and "guidings" through their "prophets."

Now the Old Testament **prophet** foretells, and often "leads." The New Testament **prophet** foretells, but never "leads." Again, New Testament PROPHETS neither foretell nor "lead." But so-called "prophets" of the "Apostolic" movement, contrary to both Testaments, "lead" but never foretell. The New Testament **prophet**, Agagbus, did not "lead": he foretold events that came to pass, and left the "leadings" to the sanctified judgement of those concerned. (Acts xi, 28; xxi, 10). The "Apostolic" "prophet" does not foretell events—he reverses the order and *forces* events by "leadings." The authority of the real **prophet** is in repeated miracles: that of the pseudo-prophet is in an affixed label.

But what about the calling of Barnanas and Paul by the prophet in Acts xiii, 1-3? Put in that way I am afraid it must be considered as a myth. This portion shows really the deliberations of a kind of local Presbytery Meeting—where two of the members were called by Holy Ghost guidance and general consent, not to an office or a title, but to a temporary task. Are not many of the presbyters in our Presbytery Meetings today prophets? And does not the Holy Ghost control their deliberations and selections still in exactly the same way? And why should the guidance here be supposed to have come through the "prophets" any more than through the "teachers" mentioned in the same verse? In any case the whole of the portion is contrary to the notion that these two servants of God were called out by a solo pronouncement of some "set prophet."

While we gratefully and joyfully admit that a **prophet** gifted by the Spirit with unmistakable miraculous revelations may still be blessedly used of God to help in times of stress and emergency, we must with equal emphasis affirm that there is no solitary case in the New Testament of seeking unto such "prophet" for "leadings"; we must also emphatically deny that possessors of the simple Gift of PROPHECY are called to fulfil any such function.

(d) The Gift is confused with Preaching.

Once again, to treat the Gift so is to rob it entirely of its supernatural character. Every translator knows well that the word for "preach" in the original is always a quite different word from the word for "prophesy." Many words in Greek are rendered by the word "preach" in the A.V. Their meaning is Proclaim, Announce, Cry. Tell—always in the sense of telling out or expounding the Word of God—The Scriptures—The

Good Tidings. Those translators who give the "preach" instead of prophesy" in English in these chapters (as in The Twentieth Century N.T. for instance) must know well that they are taking liberties with the text. Their idea is, of course, so to translate the word that they may plausibly lay claim to the possession of the Gift of Prophecy. To do so they must, since they do not believe in the miraculous, strip the word of every vestige of supernatural significance.

Preaching and prophesying are totally distinct. Prophecy is not preaching and preaching is not prophesying. In true preaching the natural mind (with its furnishings of the Word) is operated by the Spirit: in prophesying the Mind of the Spirit is speaking through natural speech organs. By an access of divine inspiration, a heavenly afflatus, preaching in the Holy Ghost may on occasion be lifted right away into the serene realm of prophecy, where every word is rich with the Spirit's breathings and winged with the Spirit's swift energy and piercing light. Preaching, in a word, is divinely inspired, but not supernatural. Prophesying is every whit supernatural. A combination of the two sets the spirit dancing, and lifts the heart to Jesus' presence.

But a good deal of what passes for preaching today is neither prophecy nor preaching in any Scripture sense; it is just a base glittering currency. a cunning counterfeit, "uttered" in the false moulds of authorized infidelity. There is no authority for preaching in the Bible. The command is to preach the Word—Jesus—The Christ—The Cross. See 2 Tim. iv; Phil. ii, 16; Acts viii, 4; xv, 35; v, 42; 1 Cor. i, 23, etc.

(e) The Gift used to be confused with the mere repitition of Scripture verses. I think this notion has almost corrected itself with experience and the passage of time. One of the offices of the Holy Ghost is to bring to our mind the Word of God (John xiv, 26); but this is a work of the Spirit through the natural faculty of memory, not through a spiritual gift at all.

The ground being thus cleared, we can now pass along to consider some Scriptural Purposes of the Gift of Prophecy.

(1) Prophecy is for speaking unto men supernaturally (xiv, 3).

In Tongues men speak to God supernaturally (xiv, 2); in Prophecy God speaks to men supernaturally—through the speech organs of men. How often a dull meeting, labouring heavily in an atmosphere too stuffily earthly and natural, has been quickened into thrilling vitality by the sudden current of heavenly prophecy! Like the free-blowing Breath of old—deep, warm, pulsating, death-chasing—that caused the skin and bones and sinews in the dry valley to glow with vigorous life before the astonished prophet who "prophesied"! How can a dry head minister water to the thirsty spirit. Fine phrases parch the soul; prophecy, like Hermon's dew, wakes the morning flowers, sets the birds singing, and starts a fountain by the way.

Beloved theologian! How can you miss this divine plan to set a flagon of heaven's wine beside your royal pieces of honest bread? Can the combination be bad, since a more bountiful than David has provided it? Bread and wine. Meat and drink. Natural and supernatural. Poise and flight. The Spirit's Word and the Spirit's Gifts.

(2) To edify the Church—the body of believers (xiv, 4).

Literally to build up. This is a good step further than speaking with tongues which just edifies ourselves. Is not the expressed purpose of the Lord Jesus to build (the same word) His Church? And if prophecy is one of His major tools in this blessed work how can we set it aside as obsolete or useless? The Written Word and the word of prophecy are complementary agents in this grand and glorious work of the Spirit (Acts xx, 32). Significantly it is among the ranks of those who look upon the Gifts of the Spirit as worn-out tools that are found great numbers who are discarding the Word also as effete and not too desirable. There are no doubters of the Word among those who believe in the Gifts of the Spirit!

To return to our first problem, let us notice that the sphere of influence of the Prophetic Gift is confined to the *Church*; the sphere of influence of the Prophetic Office may extend far beyond, even until the Prophet has become God's mouthpiece to cities, or nation's, or the whole world.

(3) To exhort the Church (xiv, 3).

Exhortation in the original signifies "a calling near." It is obviously a word of blessed meaning; to see it written (paraklesis)! is to think of the Comforter! So infused is the word with the very breath of helpfulness that the R.V. gives "comfort" instead of "exhortation," and Weymouth follows the same sweet thought in his word "encouragement." Obviously there is no inclement element of rebuke and threat to distress us here. Just the reverse, indeed. By this precious word we are really to understand those balmy words of the Holy Ghost the Comforter that encouragingly lead us away from the world and its sin and care, and "call us near" to the homely warmth of heaven and God's sweet presence.

Since I have found brethren purporting to use this precious Gift of Prophecy and its sister Interpretation of Tongues as instruments of correction in the assemblies, let me pause to say that in the New Testament, correction and rebuke come not this way but through the application of the Word in teaching and doctrine. Concerning all the improprieties and excesses that needed correction and rebuke in Corinth Paul ministered not as a prophet but as a teacher and pastor. He was indeed a prophet, even in the grand sense, but he did not stand in the Corinthian meeting pouring forth invectives and rebukes. He wrote pastoral advice, applying the Written Word of God to every problem. When he prophesied it was with blessed words of helpfulness within the meaning and the limits of this third verse.

A question may arise concerning some judgment "prophecies" I quoted under (C), page 66. There we were dealing not with a case of simple prophecy, but of prophecy being the vehicle of a Word of Wisdom. The message was a "judgment prophecy" only in the sense that it contained a warning in a prediction of events that were to take place if the warning was rejected—events that actually did come to pass, proving not merely the authority of a "prophecy" but the accuracy of a Word of Wisdom.

(4) To comfort the Church (xiv, 3, 31).

The Greek word here means consolation, solace, comfort—in trial or distress. The word "comforted" in verse 31 is the same as that translated "exhort" above; the same as that repeatedly rendered "comfort" in that lovely verse, 2 Corinthians 1, 4, "Who comforteth us in all our tribulation, that we may be able to comfort them which are in any trouble by the comfort wherewith we ourselves are comforted of God."

Is it not good to minister in divinely dictated words the solace of the Comforter to poor, suffering, sorrowing, persecuted, stumbling children of God? Wherefore, brethren, covet to prophesy! "To edification, exhortation and comfort." Such are the inspired horizons and the limits of the broad demesnes of prophecy. "Building up, stirring up, cheering up!" is Ellicott's triumphant rendering. We will do well to walk with grace and gratitude throughout the broad acres and within the fixed boundaries of this blessed inheritance.

(5) That believers may "learn" (xiv, 31).

From the position of the word here we may be sure it means that members of the Church should become wise in the mysterious supernatural beauties of the Spirit. All may prophesy, that all may learn the ecstatic delights of speaking by the Spirit—learn both by prophesying ourselves and by listening to others prophesying.

Any element of general instruction that may be suggested by this word obviously contains no mixture of distressful rebuke or correction, for it, too, is governed by this precious third verse: "to edification, exhortation, and comfort." Learning in the general sense is associated with the ministry of the teacher—not the prophet (Acts xiii, 1).

(6) To convict the unbeliever and make manifest the secrets of his heart (xiv, 24, 25).

We are proposing to discuss the problem of Tongues and unbelievers in the next chapter. In the meantime it can be said without shadow of offence to anyone that if we carefully read and re-read verses 21 to 25 we shall agree that the argument is truthfully summed up as follows: Tongues, originally intended in a secondary way as a sign to unbelievers, were, and are, rejected by them: whereas Prophecy, though intended principally for believers, has a convicting and converting influence even upon unbelievers. Inference: Employ Prophecy, not Tongues in believer's meetings where unbelievers are expected or known to be present.

So far as our purpose under this present head is concerned we can say that Prophecy serves principally for believers (22), yet since it is understood by the *mind* it may serve also as a message straight from God to the unbeliever (24, 25). Remember that Tongues, on the other hand, are not understood by the mind, but only by the spirit—and that only of the believer who speaks in them. They are thus doubly unsuitable for use in bodies of unbelievers.

But there is another sort of people coupled in these verses with unbelievers. The "unlearned". Who are these? Weymouth (and others) calls them those "who lack the gift"—that is the spiritual gift either of Tongues or Prophecy, the gifts under discussion. Wesley calls them "ignorant" persons—of course in no offensive sense. Another says, "Those who take no part in your ministrations." The Greek word means just a private person or layman: one, that is, who is "ignorant" of these supernatural things Paul is talking about—Spiritual Gifts and the Baptism in the Holy Ghost, though he might all the same be soundly saved and even learned in holy things other than the miraculous. The effect of Prophecy on these is the same as that upon sinners. "He is convinced of his sinfulness by them all [who are prophesying], he is called to account by them all; the secrets of his heart are revealed [by the supernatural *power*—as well as the words of prophecy], and then, throwing himself on his face, he will worship God, and declare, 'God is indeed among you!' " I have added the parantheses to the Twentieth Century N.T. rendering. How well I remember the first time, as "unlearned" I heard sweet words of divine prophecy! I knew God was speaking. I knew I was "out of it." Yet the very words of the prophecy persuaded me that God was intensely concerned about me, and had set His whole heart on bringing me "into it". And, Blessed be His Name—He did!

Is it not a good thing to convert the sinner to sainthood, and arrest those ignorant or sceptical of supernatural things of the Spirit, and convince them of the reality and power of miraculous Gifts? Wherefore, brethren, covet to prophesy.

In a few final observations we can briefly touch any remaining questions about use or control.

(A) We are expressly commanded to desire this particular Gift (xiv, 1) and to covet it (39). The word is exactly the same in both cases in the original and it means—as even a glance at it (zeloo) will indicate—to strive for, to be eager—enthusiastically desirous—zealous for prophecy.

Prophecy should be the Gift most commonly exercised in the Church (31), and women should prophesy as freely as men (1 Cor. xi, 5): even Joel in his prophecy of the blessed results of the outpouring of the Spirit in these latter days says, "Your sons and your daughters shall prophesy" (Joel ii, 28). Indeed, as we have already seen, in its simplest form this beautiful manifestation of the Spirit may be possessed by all (1 Cor. xiv, 1, 24, 31). And the Lord is not exclusively dependent today upon any grand order of Prophets, but might occasionally at any time convey His important revelations through the simple prophesies of His simplest prophets.

(B) Prophecy is greater than Tongues when not accompanied with Interpretation of Tongues (5); these two Gifts together, however, are equal in *value* to Prophecy. But this does not mean that Prophecy rules out the necessity of the other two. They are far from identical in purpose. Tongues and interpretation have a blessed ministry quite distinct from that of prophecy, as a glance at out chapter eleven (a) to (f) will show.

(C) Though Prophecy is clear to the understanding it is not speaking with the understanding as in verse 19: it is the Spirit of God speaking through human speech organs—it is a manifestation of the Spirit of God (xii, 7, 11).

Prophecy is divine, but it does not set aside human elements; hence its varying fluency and force in different characters: Isaiah, Amos, Jonah, Anna, Philip's daughters;

hence also its free operation through the varying speech organs of different nationalities.

(D) A believer may be endowed with Prophecy (or any other Gift) at his Baptism in the Holy Spirit, in addition to speaking with Tongues; as at Ephesus (Acts xix, 6); though there is no indication anywhere that Prophecy ever takes the place of speaking with Tongues as the initial sign of the Baptism.

(E) The Gift is not to take the place of the Written Word of God. This is most important. It is here again that the "Apostolic" movement has erred, listening to the spoken word of the human "prophet" rather than obeying the abiding Word of the Lord. How foolishly unnecessary it should be to remind ourselves that the word of man, even when he is purporting to speak for God, is always fallible, while the Word of God is always infallible! Prophecy, we are assured, shall cease (1 Cor. xiii, 8), but the Word of the Lord abideth for ever (1 Peter i, 25). Compare what was said under (C), page 172.

(F) So true is it that the Written Word is our only infallible Guide that the Scriptural character of the message in prophecy is to be judged, if necessary, by the other prophets present (29). A prophecy that is not according to the Word, or that does not fall within the Scriptural definition, is at once to be pronounced as worthless or mischievous, and repudiated without fear. (See Ezek. xiii, 1-9.) The Lord has not left His people at the mercy either of office-hunters or even genuine holders of Spiritual Gifts misusing them through ignorance or prejudice or selfishness. The Word of the Lord, not the word of the prophet, is our sure and unshakable Rock. Praise God for His precious Gifts, and for their blessed acid tests and safeguards.

There is a fault that those who prophesy often quite innocently fall into which we might mention here. The message is given an air of authority that is quite un-scriptural by the words "Thus saith the Lord" or "The Lord has spoken," or the Lord Himself is given a voice in the first person, as "I, the Lord, am in the midst" or some such words. It can be easily seen that that is flinging back responsibility upon the Lord which He has already placed upon the prophet (32). It is not the Lord who speaks, but the prophet; and the prophet speaks by the Third Person of the Trinity, not the Second. All the operations of the Gifts are manifestations of the Holy Ghost.

Let the prophet take responsibility in the Scriptural way for his own utterances, and let him frame them—not as speaking *in the place* of the Lord, but as speaking *about* the Lord. Not saying, "I, the Lord, will hear thee in the day of trouble," but as David. "The Lord hear thee in the day of trouble," or as James, "The Lord is very pitiful, and of tender mercy." It is surely wiser not to begin with the phrase, "Thus saith the Lord," and safer not to close with "The Lord hath spoken." If that were really true, how could others dare to do what the Word commands them to do, and "judge" what you have said? By our prophesying in full liberty and accepting full responsibility the Lord is glorified; moreover, He is justified in case we in our frailty utter words that are in some slight measure coloured by our anxious or wandering minds.

(G) The possessor of the Gift is responsible for its use, misuse, suppression or control.

This arises out of (F), p.173. The spirits of the prophets are subject to the prophets (32). Conybeare and Howson put it "The Gift of Prophecy does not take from the prophets the control over their own spirits." Obviously the Gift can be misused: therefore it must be regulated (29) and safeguarded (33, 40,). The prophet, not God, is responsible for any disorderly use of the Gift—however emphatically the prophet may protest he was under divine compulsion while prophesying. God is the Author of *peace*—not confusion—because He always acts and speaks in harmony with His own Written Word,

(H) The regulations for Prophecy are similar to those governing Tongues. Though all may prophesy in turn, not more than three prophecies must be given in any one meeting (29)—that is, three prophets' utterances.

(I) But though messages in Prophecy are subject to regulation they must not for that or any other reason be despised (1 Thess. v, 20). God really speaks to those who will listen. It was fear of fanaticism or disorder that in the first centuries silenced the blessed Gifts of the Spirit and left a church given over to formalism and powerlessness as a mortuary is given over to the dead. Regulations are not for suppression but stimulation. Wherefore, brethren, covet to prophesy.

(J) Messages in prohecy may often be mystical and not fully understood except in the spirits of those for whom they may be specially designed. Even the prophets of the old dispensation prophesied things beyond their own understanding, diligently seeking to know in part the meanings of their mystic pronouncements (1 Peter i, 10); so today, the Spirit's transcendent meanings are sometimes couched in sublimest terms that escape mere human thought. When Moses the Prophet of old came from the Mount of Revelation he wished not that his face was radiant with heavenly light. The shining was not for him, but for those at the foot of the Mount. In the same way his heart was laden with a burden of prophecy which he did not fully understand; which was not for him, nor principally for those to whom he spake: the precious burden was for you and me. Unto us with legal mouth he ministered those century-old wonders of Gospel grace that even "angels desire to look into"! *Mystery!*

(K) As in all the Gifts *faith* must be exercised in prophesying, and the things uttered must be within the scope of the faith possessed. "Whether prophecy, let us prophesy according to the proportion of faith" (Romans xii, 6). If we prophesy great revivals and deliverances in our assemblies that do not come to pass, then we have been prophesying beyond the proportion of our faith. There can be no blessing in that kind of prophesying.

The responsibility here is greater than in using the Gifts of Tongues, since now we are using a Gift that not only edifies the spirit but informs the mind; and further a Gift that not only profits and influences the possessor but the Church also. And more inspired courage is necessary for prophesying than for interpreting tongues, for the interpreter has a flying start, so to speak, from the unction accompanying the message in tongues while the prophet must launch out on an unction of his own. A greater measure of faith is for those reasons necessary here than for the other smaller Gifts.

(L) And finally we must ever remember that the enemy has a plan, cleverly conceived and zealously prosecuted, to destroy the supernatural, which is mightily frustrating and finally checking him (1 John iv, 4). His focal point of attack is *faith*. If he can destroy faith, even in you who possess Spiritual Gifts, he can destroy the Gifts themselves. If he can turn faith into fear he can both silence existing Gifts and prevent further heavenly bestowals. Fear is the opposite of faith (2 Tim. i, 7). It is therefore always necessary to rouse up faith, and keep rousing up faith, taking strong, bold, deliberate and determined action, if these Gifts are not to fall into disuse. Even Timothy must be warned against neglecting the Spiritual Gift he possesses (2 Tim. iv, 14), and exhorted to stir up, lest his ministry be limited by fear, and the voice of the Spirit silenced through neglect (2 Tim. i, 6, 7).

CHAPTER FOURTEEN

One Corinthians Fourteen

THE BELIEVERS' MEETING

How many people reading this chapter have taken care to note
that it is dealing exclusively with the meeting together of
Believers? Or how many of those few who have made that
discovery have further asked themselves the question, How
nearly do our own church services conform to the divine
pattern placed here for everbody to see? Could anything be
less like this pattern than the dreary deadliness of the
one-voice monotony of the Sunday meetings in the churches
and chapels we are familiar with? Is there even a breath of this
ancient fire-this heavenly utterance-this miracle atmosphere-
this soul-gripping, Christ-conscious, life-changing, God-
magnifying worship left among the dead embers of litanies and
sung eucharists and lectures and dumb silences-the matins and
evensongs and communions of today?

And if on the other hand you are at all familiar with this
Pentecostal movement and have attended a good live Breaking
of Bread meeting in a vital assembly—I ask if you could
imagine anything much *more* like this Scripture pattern than
one of those services. Which is right—Scripturally? The deadliness of the churches or the liveliness of Pentecost?

Then since it is a key to a proper understanding of this
chapter I will emphasize what I suggested in an early chapter
(Chapter Three) that not only this chapter but every one of
the chapters from ten to fourteen has for its subject the
believers' meeting for worship and Breaking of Bread. Among
other verses compare x, 16; xi, 18; xiv,6,12,19,23,26,33,and
be sure that the Lord is really giving instructions for the

proper conduct of our meetings of believers. Take the last three in reverse order. "In all churches of the *saints.*" "How is it then, *brethren?* when *ye* come together." "If therefore the whole *church* be come together." So that any instructions we get in this chapter are exclusive to that kind of meeting—the meeting where believers are convened and only believers are really expected (though an odd unbeliever might sometimes walk in unexpected and uninvited, though welcome—23, 24—"And there *come in,* one that believeth not").

Let us divide the chapter up as we did chapters twelve and thirteen, bearing in mind, however, that the problem is not just the same as in the former chapters; for here we have already given an almost complete commentary in the three chapters on Tongues, Interpretation of Tongues and Prophecy. There are, however, a few remaining thoughts we can gather up as, like Ruth with precious armfuls of grain, we pass once more over the familiar fruitful field.

1 Follow after love, and desire spiritual gifts, but rather that ye may prophesy.

2 For he that speaketh in an unknown tongue speaketh not unto men, but unto God: for no man understandeth him; howbeit in the spirit he speaketh mysteries.

3 But he that prophesieth speaketh unto men to edification and exhortation, and comfort.

4 He that speaketh in an unknown tongue edifieth himself; but he that prophesieth edifieth the church.

5 I would that ye all spake with tongues, but rather that ye prophesied: for greater is he that prophesieth than he that speaketh with tongues, except he interpret, that the church may receive edifying.

This portion gives a comparison of Tongues and Prophecy. The word "rather" in verses one and five is not used relative to the nine gifts, but to these two only—that are discussed in the chapter, and that are designed for use in the believers' meeting of which the chapter treats. This comparison between Tongues and Prophecy runs through the whole chapter. It commences in these first two verses and sums up the argument in verse 39. Though we are exhorted to covet the *best* gifts we are not encouraged to expect any specific gifts except these two-three with Interpretation. All may speak in tongues (5); all may prophesy (31); and all who speak with tongues may interpret

(13); because these three are especially designed to be employed in the believers' meeting for general ministry and mutual help. The other six gifts are not mentioned here; they are not in the same degree intended for the believers' meetings; and they do not appear in the comparison.

So far as the remaining and larger Gifts are concerned, intended as they are for a wider ministry than that exclusively of edification in assembly meetings, the Spirit will distribute these "as He will" to "covetous" believers, as He sees they may worthily bear them and profitably use them without injury to themselves (xii, 11).

6 Now, brethren, if I come unto you speaking with tongues, what shall I profit you, except I shall speak to you either by revelation, or by knowledge, or by prophesying, or by doctrine?

7 And even things without life giving sound, whether pipe or harp, except they give a distinction in the sounds, how shall it be known what is piped or harped?

8 For if the trumpet give an uncertain sound, who shall prepare himself to the battle?

9 So likewise ye, except ye utter by the tongue words easy to be understood, how shall it be known what is spoken? For ye shall speak into the air.

10 There are, it may be, so many kinds of voices in the world, and none of them is without signification.

11 Therefore if I know not the meaning of the voice, I shall be unto him that speaketh a barbarian, and he that speaketh shall be a barbarian unto me.

12 Even so ye, forasmuch as ye are zealous of spiritual gifts, seek that ye may excel to the edifying of the church.

13 Wherefore let him that speaketh in an unknown tongue pray that he may interpret.

Now the argument narrows down to a consideration of the Gift of Tongues, and the principal thought, to which the Spirit gives very patient attention and minute care, is that Tongues are designedly both intelligible and untelligible—according as they are accompanied or not accompanied with Interpretation. In private the incoherence of Tongues is no disadvantage, for the spirit understands them (2) and the mind does not need to. But in public this very circumstance renders Interpretation necessary, for the spirits of others can only be edified by Tongues as their minds are informed of the meaning through Interpretation.

Verse six shows what I have several times mentioned: the combination of Gifts in the edification of the Church. Whatever degree of revelation there may be contained in Tongues—of what use would it be to others unless some further Gift were employed with it to make these revelations known? "This being so, brothers, what good shall I do you, if I come to you and speak in tongues, unless my words (through interpretation) convey some revelation (Word of Wisdom). or knowledge (Word of Knowledge), or take the form of prophecy (in which case interpretation serves the same purpose as prophecy), or teaching (exhortation as in verse three, according to the Word of God, or instruction through the teacher's office combined with Tongues and Interpretation)?" That modern translation, with my added parentheses, I believe is a good enough explanation of verse six.

Then in verses 7-11 there are three illustrations of this need for interpretation where others are concerned. The first is from musical instruments. Musical instruments, such as flutes and harps, must do two things at once: they must give forth sound and meaning. So must these Gifts. That is the purpose of their combination, since some of the "instruments," like Tongues, are not capable alone of conveying their meanings. Then, second, martial bugles must make sense as well as sound, if others are to respond and react. I think I could myself produce a bugle's authentic sound on a bugle. But nothing would happen as the result—except perhaps a certain gratification of my personal sense of achievement. But listen to that bugler sounding the same instrument and see how perfectly he makes himself understood! The sounds are similar to mine, but now others are reacting. Men now arise and dress, or come to the cookhouse door, or fall in, or charge, or dismiss, or retire! There is meaning in the bugle because of the interpretation! So with Tongues. They are intended to move believers, but they fail without interpretation.

Then there is another beautiful figure at verses 10 and 11, a figure whose meaning is much weakened if you translate the words "voice" and "voices" as "languages"—as so many commentators do. "Language is a bad word for the word "phone" in the original, which obviously means just a sound or a voice as in our good Authorized Version. (See the same word in Revelation i, 15, His *phone* as the *phone* of many waters.) The argument is that apart from foreign human tongues there are many sounds in nature that are subtle and complex languages, but that reach our human ears as mere clucks and quacks and whinnies and tweets and baas. "For what are the voices of birds—ay, and of beasts—but words?" says the poet.

In a village in Surrey where I lived some years ago I was one day enjoying the delightful experience of watching a mother hen with her chicks. "Cluck" was all she could say, so far as I could hear. "Cluck—cluck!" But her brood got the interpretation and responded just as versatilely as children to the good English of their nurse-maids. Merrily the fluffy chicks followed their mother, stopping now and again to kick up a bit of mould backwards like mother and examine the result with one downward beady little eye. When "cluck!" the mother went again—and a miracle happened. Every little cheeping voice suddenly and completely ceased, the chicks all flocked to mother's legs and followed her in martial order into an old shed, where mother opened a dozen doors in her feathers—wherein her family silently disappeared. I was interested, not to say amazed. What had mother said? "Cluck!" was all I heard. See! . . . Aloft in the blue! Silent death! Poised wing, cruel beak, ready talon! What mother had said was really: "Children! Hawk! Hush! Quick—follow. Not a word. Now—Sh!"

And did I not hear a mother pheasant one day on brackeny moors say "Man!" as plainly as you could to her leggy brood? It must have been so, for the sweet little "voices" (phones!) became dumb in an instant, and they vanished under foxgloves and ling and never "spoke" any more, though I listened and searched for many minutes.

Do not let us think that Tongues mean nothing. Though they be nothing but "sounds" to you, they are rich languages to those enjoying the interpretation in the spirit. On the other hand, do not let us who speak with Tongues address ourselves in the presence of others in terms that cannot be understood by them. Do not let us speak into the air in Tongues, but let us rather speak to the Church through the properly appointed Gift of Interpretation. For notice that the chief end of these Gifts is the edification, not of ourselves, but of the Church (12). If we speak with other tongues—let us pray that we may interpret (13).

And should we not learn finally from these three illustrations in the portion that as we rapturously speak with Tongues God desires us to be charmed as with Seraph's flute and heaven's harps, stirred and inspired as with Michael's warrior trumpets, and informed by all the various subtleties of God's many-voiced supernature?

14 For if I pray in an unknown tongue, my spirit prayeth, but my understanding is unfruitful.

15 What is it then? I will pray with the spirit, and I will pray with the understanding also; I will sing with the spirit and I will sing with the understanding also.

16 Else, when thou shalt bless with the spirit, how shall he that occupieth the room of the unlearned say Amen at thy giving of thanks, seeing he understandeth not what thou sayest?

17 For thou verily givest thanks well, but the other is not edified.

18 I thank my God, I speak with tongues more than ye all:

19 Yet in the church I had rather speak five words with my understanding, that by my voice I might teach others also, than ten thousand words in an unknown tongue.

This portion shows the importance of balancing the supernatural with the natural, and recommends the ideal combination of the two.

Speaking with Tongues without Interpretation, we have seen, leaves the assembly unedified. And, further, speaking with Tongues entirely and exclusively, even in private, has a disproportionate effect in our beings, for it edifies the spirit only, leaving the mind barren and unprofited. We will do well, therefore, to keep a beautiful balance, neglecting neither the supernatural nor the natural: praying with the spirit—in tongues—and then changing over to the mind and praying in our own natural tongue. The same with singing: singing in tongues, in cadences provided by the spirit also, and then changing over to the hymn book and singing with the understanding the good songs of Sion.

Do not suppose that singing with the spirit is just putting plenty of fervour into our hymn-book numbers. That is singing with the understanding. As I have said before, you cannot sing with the spirit unless you speak with tongues, and you cannot speak with tongues unless you have received a miraculous Baptism in the Holy Ghost just as the 120 on the Day of Pentecost, as Paul had. And if you have never heard an ecstatic anthem to the Lord in the spirit—a thousand voices pouring out a torrent of anointed praise in heavenly languages —joining their utterances in unrehearsed music of subtlest combinations, swelling into miracle harmonies—then may the gracious Lord soon fill you with His Spirit, that you too may share in the most entrancingly lovely exercise this side heaven!

I have heard players, by a series of changing chords on organ or piano, hopelessly attempting to accompany singing with tongues in the spirit! That is indeed a hopeless and unprofitable task. In singing with the spirit not only the words are supernatural, but the melodies and harmonies also. The words uttered never were found in the singers' vocabulary, and the tunes sung never were committed to leger lines. Both are supernaturally communicated from heaven! To attempt to put supernatural words and melodies to natural chords is to reduce all to the earth plane, the natural level, and to utter confusion. It is like trying to compress the powerful tides of the River of Life within the helpless limits of our worthless earthen water-bottles!

Verse 19 does not say that speaking with tongues is a senseless and useless thing, as some pretend. It clearly means that speaking with tongues in the public assembly *without interpretation* is a selfish exercise and violates the Lord's principle of corporate and mutual edification (12); therefore when there is no interpreter the natural mind must be employed in prayers, hymns and Scripture unfoldings for others' sakes, rather than the Spirit's language to which there can be no general response.

To sum up: a proper balance must be preserved between the natural and the supernatural, both in private devotions and in the public assembly—the one for all-round individual edification, and the other for all-round corporate or Church edification.

20 Brethren, be not children in understanding; howbeit in malice be ye children, but in understanding be men.

21 In the law it is written, With men of other tongues and other lips will I speak unto this people; and yet for all that will they not hear me, saith the Lord.

22 Wherefore tongues are for a sign, not to them that believe, but to them that believe not: but prophesying serveth not for them that believe not, but for them which believe.

23 If therefore the whole church be come together into one place, and all speak with tongues, and there come in those that are unlearned, or unbelievers, will they not say that ye are mad?

24 But if all prophesy, and there come in one that believeth not, or one unlearned, he is convinced of all, he is judged of all:

25 And thus are the secrets of his heart made manifest: and so falling down on his face he will worship God, and report that God is in you of a truth.

The effect of Tongues and Prophecy on unbelievers and the "unlearned" is here compared.

And since the understanding of this is quite inseparable from a clear understanding of the passage quoted from Isaiah xxviii we will place this passage before our eyes for examination and guidance now.

Isaiah xxviii, 9-13.

9 Whom shall he teach knowledge? And whom shall he make to understand doctrine? Them that are weaned form the milk, and drawn from the breasts?

10 For precept must be upon precept, precept upon precept; line upon line, line upon line; here a little, and there a little:

11 For with stammering lips and another tongue will he speak to this people.

12 To whom he said, This is the rest wherewith ye may cause the weary to rest; and this is the refreshing: *yet they would not hear.*

13 But the word of the Lord was unto them precept upon precept, precept upon precept; line upon line, line upon line; here a little, and there a little; that they might go, and fall backward, and be broken, and snared, and taken.

In commenting on this portion in Corinthians the emphasis is invariably put on verse 22, "Wherefore tongues are for a

sign, not to them that believe, but to them that believe not."
From this a principle is deduced that "Tongues are a sign for
the unbeliever"—meaning of course that Tongues are intended
for the conviction of sinners in gospel meetings. But if we now
read again these portions from Isaiah and Corinthians, and
definitely connect them, as Paul does, we shall see that the
emphasis is really on verse 21, and especially the words: "And
yet for all that WILL THEY NOT HEAR ME, saith the Lord."
This is Paul's real text and his reasoning actually conveys the
reverse of what is generally taught.

Please look at Corinthians again. "Brethren, do not be
children in mind. As regards evil indeed be babes, but in intelligence be mature"; and link that with Isaiah xxviii, 9: "Whom
shall he teach knowledge? and whom shall he make to understand the message? Them that are weaned from the milk, and
drawn from the breasts?" . . . Babes, you see.

Now please go over what we have taken of this Corinthian
chapter and see if the following is not what Paul means: You
who are speaking with tongues in any and every kind of
meeting, without regulation or interpretation, do no be dull
and unteachable like those babes among Israel of old, who
were so ignorant that they had to be taught indeed like
infants, letter by letter, and line by line; and yet so obstinate
that even then they failed to learn what their prophets and
teachers sought to teach them, or to rectify their mistakes. On
the contrary, you Corinthians, be men, and learn from your
prophets (20, 21). Do not be children; use your reason in
reading the "Law," for therein you may clearly see that
other tongues proved useless as a means of speaking to the
unbeliever in the old days: they will prove equally useless
today. "By men of other tongues . . . will I speak to this
people, but EVEN THEN THEY WILL NOT LISTEN" (Wey.)
"Will they not say that ye are mad?" (23). Other tongues were
repudiated as a sign in Isaiah's day, and in Paul's day: they
also be repudiated in our day. This is Paul's reason for
condemning their use among sinners—and this is his purpose in
quoting the critical verse in the passage from Isaiah.

Since this question is so important, affecting the welfare of so many assemblies today, shall we examine the Scripture a little more closely? You know that this verse that Paul quotes from Isaiah (11) refers to the Assyrians whom for judgment God sent into the good Land to lay it waste. They came speaking, as the voice of Jehovah, their strange language, "with stammering lips and another tongue." They were scorned and mocked and rejected, and in that way God, too, was scorned and rejected. Their "other tongues" impressed nobody save those who, like the prophet Isaiah, were wise to God's intention, though "tongues" were not the less a sign that God was present, since the "foreigners" were there in fulfilment of God's supernaturally declared purpose. So today: though unbelievers hear the same "sign" of other tongues, they will "not hear" God therein; they will on the contrary mock and say that the speakers are mad. Only those who understand God's purpose (believers) will "hear" the sign of tongues. Therefore when sinners are present concentrate on prophecy (24), for through that precious Gift they shall hear in a tongue they *do* understand, and with an unction they cannot resist, such things as will convince them of the presence of God among you, and His judgments. The whole of chapter fourteen shows us that tongues are for the edification of the believer; to the unbeliever, if they should hear them, they are at most a judgment sign that they "will not hear—will not accept." God found other tongues futile (I speak reverently) in the conviction of unbelievers in Israel's day—so shall we today. "It is as though," says Ellicott, "the apostle said: Remember there was a time in Jewish history when an unintelligible language was sent by God, and proved *unavailing* as regards the conversion of Israel." Paul adapts this exact argument, not only to "Israel" in the sense of "unlearned," but also to "Israel" in the sense of "unbelievers," sinners. "But if all *prophesy* (blessed contrast!) and a sinner walks in—he is convinced— judged—he will fall down, worship God, and report that God is among you of a truth" (25).

So that the much misunderstood verse 22 in Corinthians xiv

really means nothing more than that tongues are a sign that unbelievers, hearing, repudiate; the unbelievers remaining unbelievers, unconvicted and unconverted, even confirmed in unbelief. "Them that believe not" refers to those who not only do not believe, but who will not believe in any case, either because of or in spite of other tongues. Tongues, even with Interpretation, have no effect on the unbeliever except to cause him to think he is listening to madmen, and further, to cause him to reject them. Can you find in the chapter any other effect than this of Tongues on unbelievers?

However you look at this argument of Paul's you must accept it as a discouragement concerning the use of tongues in a gospel meeting. For, to repeat, the whole chapter is dealing with a believers' meeting; and the only contingency Paul is entertaining at all is the possibility of an unbeliever walking unexpectedly into a *believers'* meeting and *overhearing* the use of a Gift that is intended not for him but for believers. In Paul's day, of course, there were no gospel meetings indoors like ours today. All the indoor meetings were believers' meetings. The gospel meetings were outside—as at Mars' hill for instance. Can you imagine Paul at Mars' hill among sinners speaking with tongues, and Silas interpreting him? (Acts xvii, 22)*

Another solemn lesson we learn by comparing verses 9 and 13 in Isaiah xxviii is that the stupidity of Israel—this time signifying God's people—and their unwillingness to accept "other tongues" or to learn from the lessons God had designed to teach them line upon line, eventually ruined them. Line upon line, here a little and there a little, by a backward progression, they were now in the end fallen, and broken, and snared, and taken. Have we not all seen the retrograde course of those who have as fellow believers heard the authentic voice of God in other tongues in our meetings, and tragically

---

*I personally, however, always interpret any utterance in tongues that may break in upon my preaching in a gospel meeting, on the principle that it is better to have the Gifts in manifestation anywhere than nowhere.

rejected—even loudly condemned—the voice?

And our personal experience of tongues surely bears out what we have written above. How many gospel services have we beheld quite wrecked by the unenlightened or obstinate use of Gifts that are designed only for believers! I recall for illustration a Sunday evening service that was regularly well attended by sinners listening to the gospel. Changing hands, the meeting was ruined as a *gospel* meeting in a few months by the introduction of tongues. Sinners ceased to attend. I also recall with pain how I was asked to preach the gospel at a certain assembly, and before I had chance to open my lips the meeting was ruined by eight or ten fragments of other tongues interpreted as fiery, cutting judments of God! What chance has the good tidings in an atmosphere like that? Do you think that in such conditions an assembly will *ever* get sinners into its meetings?

Concerning some large meetings where I am told tongues are employed in gospel services, I can only lovingly repeat that the practice is contrary to Scripture, and that if in God's mercy the meetings are large in spite of this unscriptural practice they would be larger without it.

One last problem remains to be considered in this section. There is an instance in the Scripture where tongues were the means of convicting those who were not yet saved. I refer to what happened on the Day of Pentecost. But the circumstances were different from Corinth, for the tongues, though unknown as they were spoken, were known as they were heard (Acts ii, 8). Now if an unbeliever, a foreigner—say a Spaniard— strayed unrecognized into a believers' meeting today (1 Cor. xiv, 23, 24). God could of course cause some saint to speak in a tongue, and further cause the tongue to be Spanish, so that the Spaniard, arrested by the miracle, would say, "How hear I this man in my own tongue, wherein I was born?" And he might further fall on his face convicted, crying, "Men and brethren, what shall I do?"—and get saved (Acts ii, 8, 37). That would be a parallel case to Pentecost, and would (as the exception provided for) be in harmony with the fourteenth chapter of

One Corinthians. And that exact thing *has* actually occurred in our assemblies more than once. But unknown tongues requiring interpretation are not for this purpose; they are for the building up of believers exclusively. Will not Pentecostal friends, in spite of present practices in the assemblies, agree that this is a fair and true setting forth of this difficult problem?

26 How is it then, brethren? when ye come together, every one of you hath a psalm, hath a doctrine, hath a tongue, hath a revelation, hath an interpretation. Let all things be done unto edifying.

27 If any man speak in an unknown tongue, let it be by two, or at the most by three, and that by course; and let one interpret.

28 But if there be no interpreter, let him keep silence in the church: and let him speak to himself, and to God.

29 Let the prophets speak two or three, and let the other judge.

30 If any thing be revealed to another that sitteth by, let the first hold his peace.

31 For ye may all prophesy one by one, that all may learn, and all may be comforted.

32 And the spirits of the prophets are subjected to the prophets.

33 For God is not the author of confusion, but of peace, as in all churches of the saints.

These verses give instructions for the conduct of the Believers' Meeting with the definite inclusion of Spiritual Gifts.

The New Testament knows of no church meeting without Spiritual Gifts and their supernatural ministry, just as it knows of no church meeting where only the one voice is heard, as in our "churches" today.

Look at the preponderance of supernatural ministry through the Gifts in verse 26! Every one is to minister his particular Gift (Romans xii, 6-8). One has a psalm—a song or a hymn in the Spirit, unlearned, unrehearsed but divinely coherent and melodious; not one of David's psalms, but one that, under the fire of divine anointing, would come out very much like David's praise songs. One has a doctrine—a real live bit of Scripture teaching or unfolding by the light of the Holy Ghost—certainly not a dull, unctionless, critical sermon. One has a tongue. (Why do they not have a tongue at your church?) One has a revelation—a showing forth of some astonishing secret of present fact or future happening, perhaps by the simple Gift of Prophecy combined with a Word of Knowledge or a Word of Wisdom; or the telling out of a heaven-sent dream or vision (Acts ii, 17). One has an interpretation—of tongues, not a dry comment out of an unanointed heart . . .

Why is not your church meeting or service like this pattern? Or why in any case should anybody be critical or alarmed at our meetings which, at least in a measure, are like this pattern?

Verse 30 may mean two things. I have already suggested it means that although many get the same revelation, only one, to obviate competition, must give it out. It also means no doubt that if a prophet is prophesying, and another "judging" learns by the Spirit that the prophecy is not according to Scripture, the one prophesying must cease speaking at the moment he is challenged!

34 Let your women keep silence in the churches: for it is not permitted unto them to speak; but they are commanded to be under obedience, as also saith the law.
35 And if they will learn any thing, let them ask their husbands at home: for it is a shame for women to speak in the church.

The behaviour of women in meetings is obviously a difficult problem, since it has divided movements and stirred shameful rancours. But there are clear rays of light here surely.

In what sense must women keep silence in the churches? Not in any absolute sense, for in verse 28 we read that men must also keep silence in the church. The special circumstances in which men are to keep silence are easy to find. It is more difficult in the case of women. But the Scripture will give us a harmonious layout of the ministry of women and their bearing in public services. There are two contexts here: first concerning the judging of prophets (29). This would not be permitted to women because it would usurp authority over the men. The second context is in verse 35. If they wish to "learn" anything arising out of any discourse "it is not permitted unto them to speak" in the meeting. They must ask their husbands not in the services but at home. The silence they are to keep concerns not giving out but taking in—not testifying but learning (1 Tim. ii, 11).

The one thing a woman must not do is to teach—that is to take a doctrinal line contrary to the teaching of the brethren in the assembly (1 Tim. ii, 12). This would not refer to those simple Bible stories and Scripture unfoldings called "teaching" in the Sunday School. All movements that have women for their heads or leaders teach error. But there is much a woman may do in public to the profit of all. She may pray in public—and prophesy (1 Cor. xi, 5), for here there is specific guidance given to women concerning God's requirements of them when they pray or prophesy in the meeting. Women may also testify (John iv, 28), and preach the gospel in public (Psalm lxviii, 11, R. V.). They may even *teach in private* if they are qualified, and at the same time accompanied by a directing male teacher (Acts xviii, 26).

Obviously all these Scriptures must be taken into account when we are trying find out the limits of women's ministry.

36 What! came the word of God out from you? or came it unto you only?

37 If any man think himself to be a prophet, or a spiritual, let him acknowledge that the things that I write unto you are the commandments of the Lord.

38 But if any man be ignorant, let him be ignorant.

39 Wherefore, brethren, covet to prophesy, and forbid not to speak with tongues.

40 Let all things be done decently and in order.

The absolute divine authority of Paul's words on the Spiritual Gifts.

They are "the commandments of the Lord" (37), and a man's claim to Spiritual Gifts is an empty one if he refuses to toe the line to absolute authority here. Commandments of the Lord are always binding; and these are neither rescinded nor modified since Paul gave them forth as from the Lord Jesus Himself. "Anyone who ignores it [the command] may be ignored" is the Twentieth Century New Testament rendering of verse 38.

Was there a "prophet" in Corinth (37) who presumptuously in his prophecies claimed revelations—as some today—superior to "the commandments of the Lord"? The best evidence of his authentic Gifts would be a reversal of his notions and a humble acceptance of this Apostolic word as it is in truth, the Word of the Lord.

Were there those also who, lifted in pride by the possession of Spiritual Gifts, considered themselves as the source of divine revelation, or the sole recipients of it (36)? Let them silence their pretended revelations and, sitting in the seat of the humble learner, submit to the written Word of God.

Brethren—whether in Pentecost or out of it—as we close our humble inquiries into this goodly supernatural Land, listen to this precious "commandment of the Lord": Covet to prophesy, and forbid not to speak with tongues.

CHAPTER FIFTEEN

Signs and Wonders and Reactions

It is generally taught by those who wish to escape inquiries on the subject that miracles occupy a very insignificant place in the Scriptures, whereas the exact opposite is the fact. Revelation is a cataract of miracles from beginning to end—a torrent so full and strong that the Bible itself is as a mighty Boulder in its supernatural current, washed by the voluminous, irresistible, overwhelming, uncapturable waters (John xx, 30, 31; xxi, 25). The combination at the head of this chapter, for instance, "signs and wonders" occurs between thirty and forty times, and the word "sign" by itself, in the sense of miracle, occurs over a hundred times. The word "miracle" appears between thirty and forty times, and "works" having the same meaning about fifty times. Then there are such words as "acts" and "doings" and others that reappear continually through the Word bearing the same significance as the word "miracle", to say nothing of the actual miracles recorded, and the miracle-prophecies and miracle-revelations where the above words do not appear at all.

The Bible indeed is a Book of Miracles. It is for that reason and many others the only Book of its sort. Why should we wish to eliminate the miraculous and bring the Bible down to the level of any ordinary history book? The Bible is even more than a Book of Miracles. It is a Miracle-Book! Not only in the sense of the things it contains, but in the real sense of the felt power emanating from it, like invisible rays eddying in irresistible arcs from a mighty city's electric generating station! Those who are filled with the Spirit with a real supernatural inrush and outburst as on the Day of Pentecost will know quite well what I mean when I say that the Bible is to the

Spirit-filled a repository of sweet influences, flowing out as they handle it, even before they begin to read it sometimes, like the rose plot that emits delicious perfume even before its fragrant site is discovered!

The Bible is a miracle zone; a supernatural demesne; a continent of wonder. The Spirit-filled child of God is habituated to its supernatural atmosphere, acclimatized to its heavenly temperatures and amazements. To him the supernatural is "natural," the unexpected is awaited, the impossible is necessary. His life is below normal if he is not repeatedly astonished. The days that record no miracles are wasted days to him. His earthly walk must constantly be visited by heaven. He belies his divine origin if his knowledge and power never break through human limits. He is different—not only morally and spiritually, but also enlightenedly and dynamically and emotionally. He sees things that only God can see; he does things that only God can do. He perceives and acts by the all-seeing and all-powerful Holy Spirit of God, as Jesus did.

The most astonishing feature of the present state of Christendom is not that Christians should be astonished at miracles, but that they should remain unastonished at the absence of them. Miracles are heaven's normalities. They were received as such in the early Church. They will be received as such again wherever there is a vital Church drenched with the Holy Spirit as at Pentecost.

Miracles react in different ways upon different classes of people. There is nothing new in this. It is all in the Scriptures. The effect of the supernatural on others is an enlightening study. Miracles react on Satan and his agents; on nominal religionists; on true believers but "unlearned" in supernatural things; on Pentecostal believers; and on unbiased sinners or "unbelievers"—producing imitations, unbelief, anger, mockery, fear, neglect, envy, ecstasy, persecution, conviction, rejection. Perhaps that sequence will form a good enough rough outline for our meditation in this chapter.

(1) First miracles react on the Adversary and his agents in such a way that for his evil ends he counterfeits them.

By "counterfeit" I do not mean pretended, like the make-believe revelations of Hananiah or certain other "prophets" in Jeremiah xiii, 14, and xxviii, 2, 10, which were just "lies" and inventions for selfish ends. Neither do I mean attempted miracles, like the essays without power of the sons of Sceva (Acts xix, 14). I mean real miracles and revelations in the power of Satan, stolen from God when, in heaven as the covering cherub, he dispensed the creative energies of Jehovah. Miracles such as were wrought by the magicians of Egypt in the presence of Moses. Or by the poor demoniac of the tombs, who by satanic force broke every fetter that his friends put upon him to protect him from self-destruction. Or the knowledge and power of the witch of Endor, or of the devil-possessed man who said to the Lord by miraculous revelation, "I know thee." In the same category are the spiritist miracles of psychism and "christian science" today: miracles that are increasing in number and astonishing power as the Day of the Lord approaches.

The purpose of these is of course to mislead suffering humanity and enlist for Satan the homage due to the Lord Jesus. The Word is full of assurance that those who "receive the love of the truth" shall not be deceived by the "working of Satan" and his "power and signs and lying wonders"(2 Thess. ii, 9), nor by the "great signs and wonders of his agents," the false Christs and false prophets who are to increase in the days before the coming of the Lord (Matt. xxiv, 24. Rev. xiii, 13, 14).

(2) Then miracles are met with distressing unbelief, both on the part of irreligious and religious people.

The irreligious, unfamiliar with the Bible, careless of any heavenly obligation or appeal, boldly deny the possibility of miracles, as the man in the moon (if there were one!) might deny the existence of dwellers on our earth! They hurt nobody but themselves. But the religious are different.They greatly hinder by their "unbelief" the miraculous deliverances and revelations of the Lord, as the men of Nazareth hindered Him in the days of His flesh (Matt. xiii, 58). The nominally religious, busy about externals and ordinances, whom the world looks upon largely as the sponsors of holy things are not only filled with unbelief but are hostile in unbelief, using in their denials neither reason nor the Word of the Lord, but the spurious authority of a crozier or a stole or a clerical collar or a divinity degree. These, like the priests and scribes and rulers of old, are envious of another's greater power, and filled with bitterness and anger. Often it would seem that if they dare they would hurl us from the brow of a hill, or destroy us as eventually they killed the Lord Jesus, infuriated by the miracles that exposed their nakedness and impotence. While we are content to quote Scripture promises and prophecies from the pulpits they will flatter us by "wondering at the gracious words that proceed out of our mouths"; but turning to mighty works, like Jesus to the miracles of Elijah and Elisha, or His own mighty works in Capernaum, they will be filled with fury and take what steps they legitimately can to move us out of their districts! (Luke iv, 22, 29). Furious anger is unhappily a common reaction to miracles still.

A more harmful class of "unbelievers" still are those who really born again but are "graciously" hostile or destructively "favourable" to the Holy Ghost and the Gifts of the Spirit; who, subscribing to some true enough but limited theological programme, resent the claims of those who have come into a later and fuller spiritual experience by the Baptism in the Holy Ghost. These are at their most dangerous when most "reasonable." They "believe" in miracles, but their faith is historic. They will not have present-day miracles, so they dispensationalize or spiritualize or naturalize them, and disown, excommunicate, commiserate, or extinguish with "faint praise" those who really believe in them. They tell us kindly that we are the "evil and adulterous generation seeking after a sign," ignoring the plain fact that those words were spoken of and to the hostile "scribes and Pharisees," and ignoring also the other plain fact that at the same time the Lord was refusing "signs" to the "evil and adulterous" He was granting them lavishly to whomsoever came to Him honestly seeking aid! (Matt. xii, 38, 39). And when the Lord said to the nobleman of Capernaum that "Except ye see signs and wonders, ye will not believe" it was not a rebuke but a statement of principle; for Jesus immediately granted him his request, showing at once both the nobleman's honesty and the Lord's ready response to his request for a "sign." And may I not—dear critical brother—repeat the Lord's words to you, assuring *you* of the same truth, that except *your* congregation see signs and wonders in this iniquitous age of unbelief they will not believe the things *you* tell them, however true they may be! Please read carefully verse 53 in John iv and see what it was that caused the nobleman and his whole house to "believe."

And be very careful of these unbelieving believers when they suavely talk in torrents about Pentecost, having no real experience of it.

"What happened at Pentecost?" asks one good brother in a popular book. "A new power of righteousness, a new mission of redemption, and a new basis of fellowship," he replies. Such generalities convey but a dark shadow of the blazing light of Pentecost. What happened at Pentecost was a new power of MIRACLES!— a new power of SIGNS and WONDERS—a new power of Christly WORKS of SUPERNATURAL HEALING according to His promise. It was not a "power of righteousness" that recommended the 120 at Pentecost but a torrent of miracle Tongues that recommended the "power of righteousness." It was not a "mission of redemption" that arrested the sinners in Samaria but a flood of mighty miracles that swept them into the "mission of redemption." It was not a "basis of fellowship" that cut the Sanhedrin to the guilty heart and put the apostles in prison for Jesus' sake; it was a new and glorious miracle wrought by fishermen that laid a Holy Ghost "basis for fellowship." Let us speak plainly the plain things in the precious Word of God. Why go round the corner to seek the truth that smacks you in the eye? Why cheat the simple with misty words? Why fling theological finesse and dialectic refinements to the hungry that are crying for BREAD? Bread, brother—Bread! Good plain honest Bible Bread! "Ye shall

197

receive POWER after that the Holy Ghost is come upon you." That is the Pentecostal Bread the hungry are looking for! Power to deliver them from the oppression, the delirium, the agony, the repulsive diseases of the devil. "They shall cast out devils, they shall speak with new tongues; they shall take up serpents; and if they drink any deadly thing, it shall not hurt them; they shall lay hands on the sick, and they shall recover." "Heal the sick, cleanse the leper, cast out demons, raise the dead." That is Pentecost! That is the kind of thing that Pentecost produced, and that is what real Pentecost will ALWAYS produce. Pentecost is the same Miracle-Working Jesus—ALIVE!—and WORKING! NOW!

Beware also of those who dwell among the half-tribes, who look across the river and say, Yes, it is good: who send out spies whose good report they receive and repeat, It is good: who climb some Pisgah and view the landscape o'er from Dan to Beersheba and exclaim, It is indeed a good land—but who do nothing about it—satisfied with a peep and a claim, instead of an invasion and an occupation. Pentecost is not a view of the land—either geographical or theological—it is a FOOT-HOLD! A POSSESSION!

Beware of those who tell you they believe in Pentecost and go on to say (as one) that "the wind and the fire and the tongues have passed, but the fellowship, etcetera etcetera, remain"! Might as well stand before Stephenson's painted "Rocket" in the museum and sentimentalize, "The fire and the water and the steam have passed—but the *reality* remains!" Where the wind and the fire and the tongues are absent, depend on it, Pentecost is absent. Where there is no super-natural breath or blaze or utterance there is positively no Pentecost. These emanations of the Holy Ghost *are* Pentecost! Pentecost is not fellowship first; there is fellowship without Pentecost. Pentecost is POWER! Supernatural Power — Unction — Miracles — Signs — Wonders — Mighty Works — Wondrous Acts — Healings — Visions — Dreams — Revelations — Prophecies — Tongues — Loud High Mighty Praises! ... LIFE!

Pentecost provides a miracle for a text for every sermon, or a sign confirming every sermon—as the Holy Spirit provided the Lord before Pentecost with a miracle for His every sermon: Bread, Light, Resurrection, Life, Cleansing, Fishing, Healing. The whole emphasis at Pentecost is placed by God on the Holy Spirit's ministry of MIRACLES! That is the meaning of the Baptism in the Spirit and the Gifts of the Spirit. And that will be the inevitable outcome of every believer's Baptism—as well as the unmistakable sign that he has received it. If you have not got supernatural manifestations, it is quite plain that you have not got Pentecost.

(3) Another reaction to Miracles and Pentecost is Mockery.

As those speaking with tongues by the Holy Ghost on the Day of Pentecost were charged with drunkenness, with its concomitants of self-indulgence and shame; as those in Corinth were charged with madness as they magnified God in other tongues; so today, we who rejoice in Christ our Saviour and praise Him in Pentecostal tongues come in for our full measure of derision and abuse.

And the very mention of the possibility of raising the dead in the power of the Spirit gives some of our critics over to unashamed and uncontrollable scornful laughter—like the pretended mourners of old! (Luke viii, 53.)

Indeed the supernatural is always mocked by the carnal, as the supernatural son Isaac was mocked by the half Egyptian Ishmael; as good Hezekiah's courageous "posts" were "laughed to scorn and mocked" as they supernaturally predicted peace from Ephraim to Zebulun; as Elisha was mocked by blasphemous youths for his part in the miracle of Elijah's translation; as many others who through supernatural *faith*, figuring prominently in heavenly miracles, have "had trial of cruel mockings . . ." (Heb. xi, 36).

(4) ". . . and scourgings, yea, moreover of bonds and imprisonment"; for Persecution is almost as common a consequence of believing in and practising miracles as it ever was in the Scriptures.

As Joseph was abused, empitted, sold, imprisoned—all

because of his faith in his supernatural dreams; as Jeremiah was flung into a foul dungeon for his supernatural predictions; as Elijah was outcast in consequence of his repeated miracles; as Micaiah was made to eat the bread of affliction in prison for his miracle-prophecy; as Samson was bound and blinded for his miracles; as the blind man at Jerusalem was cast out of the Synagogue for his supernaturally restored sight; as Paul was beaten with stripes for casting out demons; as Stephen was smashed with religious Hatred's sharp stones for seeing the Lord in heavenly splendour and daring to tell of it; as Jesus Himself was branded as an agent of Beelzebub and eventually crucified for His miracles that stripped and shamed the hypocritical priests; so today those who dare to believe in miracles in the Name of Jesus, through the Gifts of the Spirit, are derided, forsaken of friends, boycotted, abused, cast out for His glorious Name's sake. Hallelujah! And again I say—Hallelujah!

(5) And as in Stephen's day and throughout their history the nominal people of God have ever been guilty of stubbornly "resisting the Holy Ghost," so today they meet with open and shameless Rejection Pentecost and Miracles and the Spirit's supernatural outpourings and demonstrations through the miraculous Gifts.

Most Christians know how that in a great northern Convention the saints prayed earnestly for years that the Lord would pour out His Spirit as at Pentecost, and when on one glorious day the Holy Ghost actually descended in power, producing supernatural evidences of His presence all over the hall in stammerings and incoherent praises, the whole thing was checked and hushed and forbidden, until those Conventions have been swept finally clean of the Power and every trace of the Glory!

Then fear and consequent Neglect are other reactions in the presence of the supernatural; and these often among those who have been filled with the Spirit and equipped with His Gifts. But blessed be God for the great Joy and Rejoicing that, as at Samaria in Philip's day and Capernaum and elsewhere in the Lord's day, accompany the full tide of supernatural evidences and divine deliverances still! Blessed be God for the unspeakable delights of His presence still in miraculous power in our precious Pentecostal meetings.

And blessed be His holy Name that ever He brought me to know the thrill of His risen Hand upon my body, the fire of His holy Breath in my soul, and the sweetness of His heavenly Words upon my stammering tongue by the power of the mighty and ever-glorious Spirit.

CHAPTER SIXTEEN

The Need Today

THE Gifts of the Spirit are God's unfailing answer to Modernism and Formalism—those "two new cords" that have ever bound and humiliated the Spirit-filled Church of God. The Philistian shackles fly like scorched thread at the fiery touch of the Spirit!

Spiritual Gifts are an unmistakable evidence of fundamental belief in God and a simple acceptance of His inspired and infallible Word. You will never hear modernists or ritualists speak with tongues—except in high-flown classic quotations, or in the imitation gabblings in Latin that exalt the flesh and cheat the seeking sinner. You will never see the modernist or the ritualist heal the sick, for they either ignore the ordinance altogether or travesty God's appointed anointing, corrupting it into the rubbishy ritual of "extreme unction" for the dead!

What is the "church" doing for the sinner or the sick today—except send them both to the world to fare as well as they can? Is God less angry today with the shepherds that seek no lost sheep and heal no sick ones than He was in the days of the prophet Ezekiel? "The diseased have ye not strengthened, neither have ye healed that which was sick, neither have ye bound up that which was broken, neither have ye brought again that which was driven away, neither have ye sought that which was lost." God's flock is starved by those who feed themselves fat. The green pastures of His precious Word are fouled by the trampling feet of the modernist critic; the still waters that flowed from under the holy Threshold at Pentecost are fouled by the processional feet of the mockery ritualist. "As for my flock, they eat that which ye have trodden with your feet, and they drink that which ye have

202

fouled with your feet."

What is there left for God's blood-bought heritage, His spiritual Israel, His precious flock? Nothing inside the organized churches. Revival is *outside* the churches today—and will be till Jesus comes. Revival is in Pentecost—not in the glorious temples where the ritual of Pentecost is travestied still, but in the back street upper rooms where the power of the Spirit of God is mightily distributed in soul-satisfying Spiritual Gifts and outpourings. Contrast the mighty miracles and signs of the Acts of the Apostles with the banners and bands and bean-feasts of White Sunday, the churches' "Pentecost"!

But go to the despised Pentecost halls: there you will see and hear miracles and signs still; and there you will find that thirsty souls are drinking of the pure stream of the Word of God and finding life and satisfaction. The pure Word, the Saving of souls, and Miracles, are a heaven-appointed trinity inseparably joined, each member proving the remaining two, Read Mark xvi, "Preach the *Gospel* ... He that believeth and is baptized shall be *saved* ... These *signs* shall follow them that believe ... The Lord working with them and confirming the Word with signs following." The ecclesiastical trinity established by the sects is Higher-criticism, Wordly-entertainments, Powerlessness. It is only the pure Word that the Lord confirms supernaturally. Where confirmatory miracles are found you will always find the unadulterated Word. A positive absence of soul-saving and a boasted absence of miracles are the certain signs confirming the mangled Word and the corrupted ordinances of modernist and ritualist.

Please consider again that circumstance I mentioned above: The more or less authentic ritual of Pentecost was proceeding in the Temple at Jerusalem on the appointed Day of Pentecost. But the Holy Spirit ignored it all and fell in miracle torrents in the undistinguished Upper Room, sweeping every simple and unlearned worshipper into heavenly ecstasy and rapturous eloquence! Pentecost started outside the humanly guarded cloisters of professional religion. It has been outside ever since. Pentecost means the triumph of the inexpert, the unprofessional, the non-ecclesiastical. The world and the "church" want highly trained supermen. God wants cowherds and fishermen and domestics *filled with the Holy Ghost!* Pentecost is not an intensification of ability in the able: it is the imposition of power upon the utterly impotent. "Not by might, nor by power, but by my Spirit," said the Lord to Zechariah. Not by ability, nor by organization, but by the Pentecostal Baptism in the Holy Ghost. You remember Zechariah's vision was of an oil *system,* a *lamp,* and a LIGHT. Problem: Where does the Light come from? In the terms of the vision it is this: Not by golden pipes, nor by cultivated human wick—but by OIL—the Oil of the Holy Ghost, saith the Lord—whose saturate Olive Trees are rooted still in the fruitful soil of up-to-date Pentecost. Any kind of pipes will do, and any quality of wick. It is Oil that give Light, and Oil only.

In their attempts to impress and capture the unregenerate imagination the churches have elaborated their pipe systems and candelabra into a golden peep-show; but since there is no supernatural Oil there is no supernatural Light. And since there is no Light and the Bible is full of the promise of Light, they perforce must imitate the supernatural light by natural means. I saw a typical "altar" in a popular London church the other day. It had a couple of eighteen-penny electric bulbs concealed behind some fancy curtains throwing in broad day-light a wan glow over the "altar" and cross. Calling on the Corporation for the Shekinah! Tragic mockery. You must have something. If you have not got the authentic Glory in Light and Cloud and Unction, it must be simulated with tallow candles and stinking incense smoke. The Anointed Ark and the burning Altar and the naked splendour of the Cross are replaced by the floodlit reredos, the painted "altar" and the diamond-studded crucifix. What has this to do with God or His Word or sinners or salvation or the Holy Ghost? Pentecost is not parade but Power. Not show-off but Revelation. Not incense but Unction. Not sideshows but Salvation.

The ecclesiasts have turned like ungodly Ahaz to the flashy altars of Damascus; but the hand that reaches the Seraph's burning pinion is the anointed hand that has touched the blood-besprinkled Altar according to the Pattern. God does not devote His benefactions to the idols of ecclesiasticism; He does not vouchsafe the revelation of His precious things to the wise and prudent; He does not promote His salvation and His Saving Health among the dead embers of a defunct altar fire. While the withered hand of ritualism has been promoted since the Lord's day from the pew to the pulpit, the anointed hand of the Spirit-filled Nobody is today healing the sick. While the "dumb demoniac" of the Universities is struggling for utterance in the marble pulpit the anointed lips and the loosened tongue of the bus conductor are giving forth in the converted hay-loft divinely accredited Words of comfort and enlightenment and salvation and deliverance.

Christ is a Deliverer. The real *Church* of Christ is therefore a Deliverer. It was not until the Holy Spirit made it so at Pentecost. The Church of Christ is not a Lecture Course; a Social Rendezvous, a Conservatory of Aesthetics. The Church of Christ is a DELIVERER from human woe and sin and disease and despair—from Satan and hell. It can only be such by the power of Pentecost and the Gifts of the Spirit.

But why not bring the Pentecostal power into the churches as they stand? people ask. For two reasons. First, Pentecost does not consort with Bible criticism and ritualism and worldliness. Second, the churches do not wish for the introduction of a power that would sweep them clean of every vanity they cherish. It has been tried again and again. There is not a single church or denomination as such that has received Pentecost. Pentecost remains despised and rejected but all-glorious and vital "without the camp." Every individual Christian who receives his miracle-Pentecost goes ablaze with love and zeal and heavenly astonishment carrying his glowing brazier with him into his cold and dead church. Every one without exception if he presses his flaming good tidings, is evicted. The Upper Room is despised and even persecuted, by the Temple still as in the Acts of the Apostles. But it is the Upper Room and not the Temple that has the power of Pentecost.

THE GIFTS OF THE SPIRIT

Our meditations are ended; though the subject seems barely touched. The Gifts of the Spirit are the evidences and expression of the indwelling Spirit. Did you receive the Holy Spirit when you believed? Paul did not—nor the Samaritans—nor the "120" at Jerusalem. But they all received some little time afterwards. So may you. They received because they sought. Have you sought? They received because they would not be put off with a "faith" Baptism. They would not be content with less than a Power Baptism. Their Baptism in every case was evidenced and ratified by a miracle: they spake with tongues according to the plan and promise of the risen Jesus. They continued to testify and minister in miraculous power till the Lord came to carry their spirits home. Pentecost means miracles by the Gifts of the Spirit. Continued Pentecost means continued miracles by the continued operation of the abiding Spirit. The manifestation of the Spirit is given to every man who is filled with the Spirit. Have you received your supernatural manifestation?

Sinners are going daily to everlasting perdition for lack of truth and power in the ministry of the Word. The sick are choking in agony in spite of the hospitals for lack of one to heal them. The sorrowful are destroying themselves in increasing numbers for lack of the comfort the Comforter can bring. All have turned from the churches—because the churches have turned from the Lord. The heart of the world is hungry and crying aloud for Bread. Give ye them to eat. You can do it in the power of the Baptism and through the agency of the Gifts of the Spirit. Take up the instruments that Paul laid down when he laid down his life for Jesus' sake. Take up the instruments that made the early Church mighty in God. Take up the instruments that Jesus used—that He promised to all who should believe for them—that will still accomplish all that He accomplished for suffering and sinful humanity, and that will continue to bring Him glory in the loud praises of the delivered.

"Thou that dwellest between the cherubims, shine forth. Stir up thy strength. Come and save us. Cause thy face to shine; and we shall be saved. Give light to them that sit in darkness. Give power to the faint. Increase power to them that have no strength. Open the blind eyes, O Thou who givest breath to the people upon the earth, and spirit to them that walk therein; bring out the prisoners from the prison. Let the inhabitants of the rock sing, let them shout from the top of the mountains. Let them give glory unto the Lord, and declare His praise. *Who among you will give ear unto this?* Who will hearken and hear for the time to come?" (Psalm lxxx, etc.).

May you who are His truly hearken, until you can "fully preach the gospel of Christ, by word and deed, so that mighty signs and wonders are wrought by the power of the Spirit of God" (Romans xv, 18, 19, 20).

May you who are thirsty in the denominations, as I was, come to the Living Water that you may find rivers for refreshment and overflow.

And may you who are already in Pentecost, Cry out and shout—inhabitants of *heaven!*-for great is the Holy One in the midst of thee. Hallelujah!

Now unto Him that is able to do exceeding abundantly above all that we ask or think, according to the power that worketh in us, Unto Him be glory in the church by Christ Jesus throughout all ages, world without end. Amen.